Regional Innovation Potential: The Case of the U.S. Machine Tool Industry

STEVEN R. NIVIN

Routledge
Taylor & Francis Group

LONDON AND NEW YORK

First published 2000 by Ashgate Publishing

Reissued 2018 by Routledge
2 Park Square, Milton Park, Abingdon, Oxon OX14 4RN
711 Third Avenue, New York, NY 10017, USA

Routledge is an imprint of the Taylor & Francis Group, an informa business

Copyright © Steven R. Nivin 2000

Notice:
Product or corporate names may be trademarks or registered trademarks, and are used only for identification and explanation without intent to infringe.

Publisher's Note
The publisher has gone to great lengths to ensure the quality of this reprint but points out that some imperfections in the original copies may be apparent.

Disclaimer
The publisher has made every effort to trace copyright holders and welcomes correspondence from those they have been unable to contact.

A Library of Congress record exists under LC control number: 00131255

ISBN 13: 978-1-138-71709-1 (hbk)
ISBN 13: 978-1-138-71708-4 (pbk)
ISBN 13: 978-1-315-19652-7 (ebk)

Table of Contents

List of Figures

List of Tables

1 Introduction

Introduction

This study analyzes a process vital to economic development - technological change. It is an attempt to further understand the processes driving innovation, so that we may gain a deeper insight into the development of economies. Specifically, the study explores the concept of *innovation potential* and the factors that result in variations in innovation potential across metropolitan areas, using the U.S. machine tool industry as a case study.

Innovation Potential

Given the importance of innovation potential in economic development, it is essential to know what influences the development of this potential. Borrowing from a similar conception of innovative capacity developed by Suarez-Villa (1993), innovation potential will be operationalized as the number of United States machine tool patents granted from 1990 through 1992 across metropolitan areas. Suarez-Villa had defined innovative capacity as the sum of all patents across multi-state regions over a seventeen year period. The measure used here provides more geographic detail for a less aggregative time period, thereby creating a measure of both the urban region's ability to invent and its potential to innovate.

While not all inventions[1] are patented and not all inventions become innovations,[2] patent data is a reliable measure of invention (Acs and Audretsch, 1989; Basberg, 1987; Boitani and Ciciotti, 1990; Comanor and Scherer, 1969; Griliches, 1990; Griliches, Pakes, and Hall, 1987; Narin, Noma, and Perry, 1987; Pakes and Griliches, 1984; Suarez-Villa, 1993). Since

---

[1] Invention is "the discovery of basic scientific and technological knowledge" (Suarez-Villa 1993, 148).

[2] Innovation is "the application and development of inventions in ways that may directly determine economic change" (Suarez-Villa 1993, 148).

invention is the precursor to innovation, the more inventions created the greater the potential that some of them will register an economic impact as innovations. Hence, the use of patent data in this study should provide an adequate measure of regional innovation potential.

Innovation potential has a significant impact on the rate of growth and development of an economy. It is of interest to know what influences the development of this potential. Innovation potential can be derived from both indigenous and exogenous sources. The indigenous sources of innovation potential include the institutions, infrastructures, social systems, and stocks of human capital present within the economy. The influence of exogenous sources depends on the capacity of economic agents to be creative adaptors of fundamental innovations imported from elsewhere. This study focuses on the influences of the indigenous sources.

The Sectoral Dimension

It seems plausible that these indigenous influences can have varying degrees of impact on the innovation potential of the industries within a region (Malecki, 1991; Porter, 1990; Suarez-Villa, 1993; Suarez-Villa and Hasnath, 1993). The focus of this study is sharpened by analyzing the factors influencing the innovation potential of one industry - the United States machine tool industry.[3]

This industry is of interest "because machine tools are the foundation for almost all of manufacturing" (Ashburn, 1988, p.19). In other words, the machine tool industry is the provider of all the capital goods upon which the manufacturing sector is so dependent. This means that this one industry sets the bounds or parameters for the performance of other industries. Since capital goods embody the state of technology, the more sophisticated the products of the machine tool industry, the more sophisticated the products of other manufacturers can be.

---

[3] By framing the discussion in terms of the innovation potential of the machine tool industry, it is not meant to imply that all of the patents produced within the region were created only by inventors within a machine tool firm. Some of the patents were granted to inventors not associated with a firm, or at least, the patent did not have a firm as the assignee. Either way, the invention adds to the innovation potential of the machine tool industry.

Machine tools is a nodal industry. It is the transmission point of new technology to the rest of manufacturing industry. An innovative and competitive machine tool industry contributes significantly to the rapid diffusion of new technology and to the realization of the competitive benefits that this makes possible for the rest of manufacturing industry (Sciberras and Payne, 1985, p.63, quoted in Ashburn, 1988, p.20).

Ultimately, then, it is innovation within the machine tool industry that allows the manufacturing sector of the economy to innovate and reap the competitive benefits, which gives the machine tool industry its importance. The need for an innovative machine tool industry, combined with the fact that innovation requires a constant source of new knowledge (i.e. invention patents), imposes on us the need to know where this new knowledge is created and the factors that make some metro-regions more conducive to inventive activity within this industry than others.

Innovation Potential and Regional Economic Development

The innovation potential of regions plays a significant role in their growth and development (Brugger and Stuckey, 1987; Griffin, 1978; Grossman and Helpman, 1994; Landau, 1988; Malecki, 1991; Ogburn, 1933; Quinn, 1986; Romer, 1986; Romer, 1994; Rosenberg, 1986; Schmookler, 1966; Schumpeter, 1950; Solow, 1957; Stewart, 1978; Suarez-Villa, 1993; Suarez-Villa and Hasnath, 1993; Westphal, 1987). It is technological change, according to Schumpeter (1950), that causes the creative destruction which drives the capitalist economy. Increasing innovation potential within a region can spawn the new industries, make existing ones more efficient, enhance the international competitiveness of the region, and attract highly skilled labor catalyzing economic development (Suarez-Villa, 1993; Suarez-Villa and Hasnath, 1993). Thus, those economies whose innovation potential lags will also lag in the rates of growth and development they experience: "the innovation gap among regions is a primary source of regional development disparities..." (Malecki, 1991, p.28). But what is meant by a *regional* economy? How is a regional economy defined in this study?

3

The Spatial Dimension

Although regional scientists have struggled for many years trying to find the most appropriate definition of "region", a consensus has yet to be reached. Regions have historically had three different definitions: (1) areas that are homogeneous physically, socially, or economically, (2) nodes around a central urban economic center, and (3) areas defined by political boundaries (Meyer, 1963). Markusen (1987) defines a region as

> an historically evolved, contiguous territorial society that possesses a physical environment, a socioeconomic, political, and cultural milieu, and a spatial structure distinct from other regions and from the other major territorial units, city and nation (Markusen, 1987, pp.16-17).

Gilbert (1988) provides a synopsis of the concept of region as defined by English and French-speaking regional scientists. There are three definitions. First, region is defined "as the spatial organization of the social processes associated with the mode of production" (Gilbert, 1988, p.209). Second, "the region is defined as a specific set of cultural relationships between a group and particular places" (Gilbert, 1988, p.210). Third, the region is conceptualized "as a medium for social interaction" (Gilbert, 1988, p.212). This last definition is essentially the region defined by political boundaries. Hence, it is evident that the concept of region presents a difficult definitional dilemma for regional scientists.

Being unable to agree upon a single all-encompassing definition of region, regional studies have used the full spectrum of geographic definitions of region as their unit of analysis. Such studies have used definitions of region ranging from large multi-state regions to the relatively smaller metropolitan areas. What is the appropriate spatial conceptualization for this study?

In a study similar to this one, but using states as the geographic unit of analysis, Feldman (1992) writes: "States are not an entirely satisfactorily unit of observation to use in this analysis.... Ideally, we would like data at a sub-state level of aggregation" (Feldman, 1992, p.9). If the state is not an appropriate unit of analysis, it appears reasonable to argue that the larger multi-state region would also not be the most suitable. Furthermore, an even larger region - the nation - would appear to be even more inappropriate. As Porter states, "the importance of geographic concentration raises interesting questions about whether the nation is a relevant unit of analysis" (Porter, 1990, p.157). Furthermore, states and nations are not suitable units of analysis because they are defined by political boundaries and "regions are decidedly not well defined by political boundaries" (Malecki, 1991, p.9) because they have not evolved out of natural economic processes. Thus, such definitions are not only awkward in a study of the influences of regional economic inputs, but they fail to capture the benefits of the clustering or agglomeration of these inputs that are so pervasive in advanced economies (Porter, 1990, p.149).

It becomes evident that the metro-region is an appropriate unit of analysis when one views the geography of economic activity. For example, according to Hicks and Rees (1993), the 300 U.S. metropolitan areas contain 19.7% of the land area in the country, but 77.7% of the nation's population lived in these regions. Furthermore, during the decade of the 1980s, 90.1% of the population growth within the U.S. occurred within metro-regions (Hicks and Rees, 1993, pp.2-4). As employment centers, 80.8% of America's employment was located in metro-regions in 1990 - an increasing share compared to 1970 (79%) and 1980 (79.3%). These regions also accounted for 87.2% of the employment growth within the nation during the 1980-1990 decade (Hicks and Rees, 1993, pp.2-7). In sum, metro-regions are the central market for labor (Berry, 1973) as well as being the hubs of economic activity throughout the country.

This is also true for inventive activity within the machine tool industry. As shown in Table 1.1, of the 9,736 machine tool patents granted to American inventors from 1976 through 1992, 8,529 (87.6%) of them were granted to inventors residing within metropolitan areas.

Table 1.1-Machine tool patents granted in the U.S., 1976-1992

Residence of Inventor	Patents (#)	% of Total	% of Domestic
Total	17,129	-	-
Domestic	9,736	56.8	-
Foreign	8,193	47.8	-
Within Metro-Regions	8,529	49.7	87.6

Source: U.S. Office of Trademarks and Patents

These statistics provide evidence that metro-regions are the centers of economic activity within the United States. The vast majority of economic activity occurs within these regions. They benefit from the agglomeration of resources and the technological and functional linkages and interdependencies flowing out of the clusters of economic activity[4] (Abernathy and Utterback, 1978; Carlino, 1987; Carlino, 1993; Czamanski and Ablas, 1979; Feldman, 1992; Hicks and Nivin, 1993, 1994, 1995, 1996; Krugman, 1991; Malecki, 1991; Porter, 1990). Metro-regions can provide a better approximation of an area evolved out of economic processes that contains the "socioeconomic, political, and cultural milieu" required of Markusen than either states or multi-state regions. Use of the metropolitan area as the unit of observation satisfies at least one definition of region and focuses the study on the places in space where almost all of the economic activity within the United States occurs.

Research Questions

The U.S. machine tool industry is vital to the performance of domestic and global manufacturing. It   provides the stock of capital goods which embody the new production technologies upon which manufacturing is dependent. The innovation potential of the U.S. capital goods industry creates a stock of patented inventions upon which manufacturing can draw to make itself more competitive.

Given the importance of this industry and the influence that invention can have on economic growth, this study provides answers to the following questions:

(1) How is the innovation potential of the machine tool industry organized spatially and temporally?

(2) What factors account for the spatial and temporal organization in this industry's innovation potential?

Comparison of answers to question (2) with answers to the same question posed with respect to the semiconductor industry will provide at least a partial solution to a third research question:

---

4 For a more detailed discussion of agglomeration economies, see chapter three or the aforementioned cited works.

(3) Are the factors that influence spatially- clustered innovation potential industry-specific?

Why this comparison? The machine tool industry is an older, established industry, and the semiconductor industry is a relatively younger, rapidly growing industry that performs many similar functions with respect to the Information Age economy. Comparing the determinants of the innovation potential of these two industries should provide insights into whether there are common forces driving differences in innovation potential, or whether understanding must be industry-specific.

Overview

This study is organized as follows. Chapter two provides a historical perspective, briefly tracing the development of the machine tool industry from its birth to the present, emphasizing the technological advances that have facilitated its growth. Chapter three reviews the literature dealing with the factors that stimulate invention. Chapter four lays out the structure of the analysis. Innovation potential is modeled as a function of urbanization economies, localization economies, federal government demand-pull, human capital, industrial restructuring, information technology investment, and invention-derived knowledge (IDK). For comparative purposes, a model of semiconductor innovation potential is designed. Chapter five outlines the process of trial and error by which statistical problems were encountered and resolved, presents the principal findings, and considers whether the conclusions are industry-specific. Finally, chapter six gives overviews of the conclusions, considers the policy implications, and explores avenues for future research.

2 The Development of the Machine Tool Industry

The Early Industry: Emergence to the Early 1900s

John Wilkinson developed the first machine tool in England in 1774. He developed a boring machine that was vital to the production of the steam engine because it made it possible to produce the cylinders in the Watt steam engine. The first machine tool patent granted in the United States went to David Wilkinson (no relation to John Wilkinson), for his invention of the screw-cutting lathe, twenty-five years after the boring machine of John Wilkinson. Thus, David Wilkinson is considered to be the father of the machine tool industry in the United States (*American Machinist*, 1977, p.B-4).

Until approximately 1840, individual machine tool companies did not exist. Before this time, if a company needed a machine tool, they were forced to design and build it themselves. There was no company in existence whose main purpose it was to build and sell machinetools to other manufacturers (DiFilippo, 1986, p.16). In fact, the formation of independent machine tool makers began in earnest from 1840 to 1880.

> The growth of independent machinery-producing firms occurred in a continuing sequence of stages roughly between the years 1840-1880. These stages reflect both the growth in the size of the market for such machines and the accretion of technical skills and knowledge (and growth in the number of individuals possessing them) which eventually created a pattern of product specialization by machine-producing firms which was closely geared to accommodating the requirements of machine users (Rosenberg, 1963, p.418).

In other words, the birth and development of the machine tool industry in America was closely tied to the skilled human capital available and to the demands of several industries.

The arms makers played a key role in the birth and development of the machine tool industry. While legend holds that the first demand for interchangeable parts in weapons bought by the government was in a contract given to Eli Whitney in 1798, the earliest evidence of such demands is found in a contract granted to Simeon North in 1813. The demand by the United States government that these weapons be made with interchangeable parts is important because it provided the impetus to develop the necessary machine tools, for without these tools it was impossible to achieve interchangeability. It is just too difficult to hand file parts to certain specifications so as to make them interchangeable, and it is certainly impossible to achieve this on a mass scale. This problem was solved with the invention of the milling machine (Ashburn, 1988, p.24). Thus, the requirements of the armories led to the development of machine tools that were lighter, more specialized, and higher-speed than those produced as a result of the requirements of the textile industry (Rosenberg, 1963, p.419).

The developments resulting from the demands of the armories resulted in the American System of Manufactures. In fact, "how the 'American system' developed is the story of the real birth of the machine tool industry" (Ashburn, 1988, p.23). In 1853, the armory of Robbins and Lawrence received a contract from Britain to build 25,000 Enfield rifles as well as equip a new British armory with 157 machine tools. While Robbins and Lawrence did not consider themselves to be machine tool builders, the order was a turning point in the development of the industry.

While Lawrence was not successful in his efforts to get the Sharps Company (which now owned the Robbins and Lawrence plant in Hartford) to become a machine tool company, others did start to establish independent machine tool companies. Many of these entrepreneurs spun-off from the armories where they gained what was probably invaluable experience with the design, manufacture, and use of machine tools. In fact, the Colt armory was a particularly good source for these entrepreneurs. Another source of independent machine tool firms was the general machine shops present in New England at this time. "Such shops did not produce standard machines and go out and sell them: they innovated on demand" (*American Machinist*, 1977, p.C-1).

Also playing significant roles in the early development of the machine tool industry were the sewing machine, bicycle, and automobile industries. "The sewing machine industry was the first to build on the manufacturing system developed by the arms makers" (Ashburn, 1988, p.31). The bicycle industry provided the biggest boost to the machine tool business in the last decade of the nineteenth century and the first decade of the twentieth century. The strong demand for machine tools by the bicycle industry led to several machine tool innovations, such as the grinding machine, as well as improvements in other equipment.

While the bicycle industry began its decline at the beginning of the twentieth century, the automobile industry arrived and more than adequately filled the void in demand, becoming the largest consumer of machine tools by World War 1. The requirements of the automobile industry induced several significant innovations in machine tools, particularly in the case of grinding machines. For example, a grinding machine was invented by Franklin Norton in 1903 that was capable of grinding an automobile crankshaft in only fifteen minutes. The camshaft grinder was invented in 1911; the internal grinder, invented in 1905, was used to produce cylinders with walls that were of superior straightness, and to grind the piston rings, the disk grinder was invented in 1891. Yet another example is the creation of the production centerless grinder introduced by the Cincinnati Milling Machine Company in 1922 which was used by the automobile industry in grinding parts like pushrods and valve tappets. Besides innovations in grinding, "other major machine tool improvements or innovations occurred in milling, in tapping, in the lathe, and in drilling owing to the enormous growth of the automobile industry" (DiFilippo, 1986, p.22).

It seems clear, then, that the birth and early development of the machine tool industry was closely tied to the birth and development of other industries. As Rosenberg states,

> ...the machine tool industry itself was generated as the result of the specific production requirements of a sequence of industries which adopted techniques of machine production throughout the period. In each case, the introduction of a new process or a new product required an adaptation and adjustment in the capital goods industries to new technical requirements and specifications which did not initially exist. There took place, as it were, a period of technical gestation at the intermediate stages of production, during which time the appropriate accommodations were made to the specific technical needs of the new process or product. As the demand for particular kinds of machines became sufficiently great, reflecting the fact that the same machines came to be employed in a progressively increasing number of industries, the production of that machine itself came to constitute a specialized operation on the part of individual establishments.

The machine tool, then, originated out of a response to the machinery requirements of a succession of particular industries; while still attached to their industries of origin, these establishments undertook to produce machines for diverse other industries, because the technical skills acquired in the industry of origin had direct application to production problems in other industries; and finally, with the continued growth in demand for an increasing array of specialized machines, machine tool production emerged as a separate industry consisting of a large number of firms most of which confined their operations to a narrow range of products - frequently to a single type of machine tool, with minor modifications with respect to size, auxiliary attachments, or components (Rosenberg, 1963, pp.420-421).

Placing an actual date on the birth of this industry is a debatable affair. It appears, as Ashburn would argue, the industry was born with the spin-off firms from the armories in the second half of the nineteenth century. Other evidence seems to support this. The metalworking trade journal, *American Machinist*, published its first issue in November 1877, indicating some semblance of a machine tool industry. Furthermore, this same trade journal published a list of machine tool companies in their June 28, 1879 issue and even went so far as to claim these firms were 'a distinct branch of industry' (DiFilippo, 1986, p.21). One could also argue that the industry was born in 1902 with the formation of the National Machine Tool Builders' Association. Either way, "it is clear that no distinct machine tool industry existed in America prior to 1877" (DiFilippo, 1986, p.21), and since the latest possible date is 1902, it at least seems reasonable to say the machine tool industry began sometime between 1877 and 1902 (DiFilippo, 1986, p.21).

The birth of the machine tool industry was, in large part, due to technological advances and the forces that propelled these advances. Demand from numerous industries probably had the most significant influence, with the largest impact being derived from the auto industry. Other influences that were important include the development of skilled labor through apprenticeships and the close relationships between machine tool makers and their customers, allowing for important transfer of information, and learning by using.

Technological Advance and the Growth of the American Machine Tool Industry: 1890s to 1970s

Two major technological leaps played a leading role in propelling the U.S. machine tool industry into a worldwide leadership position: (1) the development of high speed steel and the use of the electric motor and (2) the invention of numerically controlled and computer numerically controlled machine tools.

High Speed Steel and the Electric Motor

Frederick W. Taylor was working at Midvale Steel Company when he began his experiments on the composition of tool steel in 1890. Having clashed with Charles Harrah, Jr., the president of Midvale, over his experiments with tungsten, an ingredient not produced by Midvale, Taylor resigned. He later joined Bethlehem Steel and began working with Maunsel White in 1898. In 1900, they developed the Taylor-White process whereby they produced the first high-speed steel. This development, displayed at the Paris Exposition of 1900, rendered every machine tool in the world obsolete.

While the first use of electric motors to drive machine tools dates to 1892, Taylor used electric motors to drive the machine tools in his experiments beginning in 1894. In fact, high-speed steel tools required greater amounts of power than previous tools, and electric motors were a good source of this greater power. It was also thought that electric motors would use less energy than the lineshafts, countershafts, and jackshafts driving most of the machine tools of the day. Even with these advantages, widespread use of electric motors did not occur until the 1920s, and adoption of high-speed steel tools was quite slow as well. The reasons for the slow rate of diffusion were both economic and technical. Economically, when the number of jobs were small, it was not prudent to use high-speed tools given the high extra cost of the tools. Technically, the electric motors transmitted vibrations to the tools that made it extremely difficult, if not impossible, to put a fine finish on a surface when necessary. Thus, grinding machines were the last machine tools equipped with electric motors.

It was three Frenchmen who are credited with first controlling a machine tool by inputting stored digital data. In 1906, the Sellers company built a machine that could punch rivet holes in sheets and angles of steel up to ten feet wide and one hundred feet long. The pattern of the holes to be punched was fed into the machine through a pattern of holes punched on a paper tape similar to the way instructions are fed into a player piano. Although none were ever built, Emanual Scheyer, in 1921, designed a machine that was to be entirely controlled by a tape similar to the one in the Sellers machine.

It was the Jacquard loom, though, developed in 1804, which was actually the first machine created with the ability to be programmed. As was done with the first numerically controlled (NC) machine tool developed at the Sellers company, the loom was programmed in a similar manner to that of a player piano. Thus,

> in a sense, all subsequent programmable machines are the fruit of the loom. It was the technology of the Jacquard loom, with its ability to turn abstraction into physical patterns, that inspired early forays into the automation of machine tools after the second world war (*The Economist*, 5 March 1994, p.6).

It was, therefore, an invention in another industry that facilitated the development of numerically controlled machine tools.

John T. Parsons was the person who really set the development of numerically controlled machine tools on its true course. After seeing the proposed designs for an airplane to be built by Lockheed featuring integrally stiffened skins, Parsons inquired about how the plane was to be built. He thought the methods proposed to be impractical and thus, set out to create a more practical method. The method he had in mind was one in which the data was fed to a milling machine through punched cards.

He interested the Air Force in his idea and signed a contract to develop such a machine on June 15, 1949. IBM agreed to develop the card reader, and the machine was to be built by Snyder Tool and Engineering Company, a Detroit machine tool manufacturer. Parsons' personal downfall was giving a subcontract to Servomechanisms Laboratory at MIT because they were interested in producing a continuous-path control system. MIT eventually pushed Parsons out and signed their own contract with the Air Force. Soon afterwards, MIT was demonstrating its development of numerical control.

The machines were not too economical because of the high cost of programming the machines. Because of this, the Air Force sponsored a project that included nineteen aircraft firms whose purpose was to develop automatically programmed tools. But, like the system developed by MIT, it was very complex and expensive. Private industry was extremely reluctant to invest in these new machines, so it was in the hands of the Air Force to provide the catalyst for their further development, which it did with orders for one hundred five-axis continuous-path milling machines.

Having developed the machines in a laboratory at MIT, all involved in the project were in for an eye-opening experience when the first machine under the Air Force contract was installed in 1958. The manufacturing floor was a much different environment than the laboratory and provided the developers with numerous problems. The developers had not taken into consideration the vibration, electrical interference, and contaminants in the air of a factory. They also ran into problems of plant maintenance personnel who were inexperienced with the electronically controlled machines and operators who did not know how to properly handle the tapes. Needless to say, the diffusion of these machines was difficult at first.

Other developments in numerical control were also taking place during the time of the development of the MIT machine. Frederick Cunningham, working for the Arma Corporation, developed a digitally controlled lathe, which was demonstrated in 1950. The visionary responsible, in large part, for the commercial success of numerically controlled machine tools was Adrian Holmberg. He was one of the first people to understand the commercial advantages of such machine tools and urged their development. He was quite successful, for there were more than one hundred numerically controlled machine tools on display at the 1960 machine tool show, and his own company, Miehle-Goss-Dexter had twenty-two numerically controlled machine tools in operation themselves.

As numerically controlled machine tools developed, advances led to the creation of machining centers and turning centers. A machining center could perform the tasks requiring standard milling, drilling, and boring machines as well as tasks normally requiring a lathe. It would allow four sides of a piece to be worked on in one set-up, and changing tools was relatively quick.

The turning center was created by adding turrets to numerically controlled lathes so as to allow programmed tool changes. Later, powered tool positions were added to the turrets to allow milling and drilling operations to be performed on the turning center. These turning centers, along with the machining centers, became a significant portion of machine tool output relatively quickly.

Illustrating, yet again, the influence of an invention in another industry on the technological advance in the machine tool industry is the creation of the computer. The computer allowed machine tool makers to advance the state of the art of machine tools from the difficult methods of programming the machines through punch tapes to the ease of programming provided by computer software. This technology was first displayed on a widespread basis at the Chicago machine tool show in 1970 (*American Machinist*, 19 October 1970). While the United States pioneered the development of NC and computer numerically controlled (CNC) machine tools, it was their foreign counterparts that thoroughly seized the opportunities provided by these new technologies. In fact, it is the introduction of CNC and the failure of the American machine tool industry to seize upon this opportunity that marks the precipitous decline of the preeminence of the American industry in the international arena.

Crisis or Creative Destruction: 1980s to 1990s[1]

At the beginning of the 1980s, America's machine tool industry was the largest in the world, but the decade of the eighties would be one of precipitous decline. Virtually every product market experienced a loss in domestic market share, with only a very few experiencing growth, and that due to the protection they received.

> Germany and Japan have become the world's leading machine-tool producers. The U.S. share of world markets dropped from 20 percent in 1980 to just over 7 percent a decade later, at the same level as Italy, whose

---

[1] This section was drawn from the following sources: Ashburn (1988), Dertouzos et al. (1989), DiFilippo (1986), Finegold et al. (1994) and Rendeiro (1985).

economy is less than one quarter the size of the U.S. economy. The loss of U.S. machine-tool competitiveness was most evident in the domestic market, where imports surged from 24 to 54 percent of total U.S. sales in just seven years. As a consequence, the historical U.S. trade surplus in machine tools evaporated, giving way to a trade deficit of $1.7 billion in 1986. With this drop in competitiveness, the size of the U.S. machine-tool industry was cut in half. Production in 1991 was just 42 percent of its 1980 level; total employment declined from 108,000 to 53,300 between 1980 and 1992, with the number of production workers dropping from 71,100 to 32,800 (Finegold et al., 1994, pp.11-12).

What caused the decline? Was the U.S. machine tool industry truly in a crisis and on the brink of extinction, or was this a classic case of Schumpeterian creative destruction?

Several factors have been cited to explain the decline: (1) a declining domestic market, (2) growing international competition, (3) ownership by large conglomerates, (4) shortage of skilled labor, (5) industry structure, (6) lack of innovation and slow diffusion of high-impact innovations, (7) the industry's response to the business cycle, (8) short-term perspective of the financial community, and (9) government policies and regulation. Several of these causes are also reasons as to why the industry was so slow to respond.

A Declining Domestic Market

The domestic demand for machine tools declined by 37% in the decade of the 1980s (Finegold et al., 1994, p.18). The use of plastics and other materials in the place of metal and process improvements, decreasing the need for machine tools, have played a significant part in the decline of the market (Dertouzos et al., 1989, p.235). Having such a large domestic market, the U.S. machine tool industry became dependent on this market. Since this market has shrunk, having such easy access to a market of this size has proven to be a curse rather than a blessing since it has worsened the impact of the decline of the domestic market. Furthermore, the industry was not oriented toward the export markets, so there was nothing to cushion the blow of a shrinking domestic market.

While machine tool demand declined during the 1980s, this was not a worldwide phenomenon. For example, Germany and Japan became the largest machine tool consumers in the world by 1991, and regionally, Europe and the Pacific Rim have become the largest markets. In fact,

> The European Union, accounting for 34 percent of world consumption, is the largest single integrated machine-tool market in the world; the Pacific Rim is the fastest growing regional market (Finegold et al., 1994, p.66).

The American machine tool industry was ill-suited to adapt to this shift in global demand for several reasons.

First of all, the industry was oriented more to the domestic market than to the export market. Since America's machine tool firms had a captive domestic market large enough to keep them near full capacity, they paid little attention to the international market. They would export during a downturn in the business cycle, but once the domestic market recovered, they would neglect their international customers (Finegold et al., 1994, pp.68-69). The geographic clustering of the industry tended to strengthen the emphasis on the domestic market by providing the firms with a regional focus (Dertouzos et al., 1989, p.237).

Compounding this problem is the fact that neither the U.S. government nor the professional associations provide support or guidance to those firms interested in exporting their tools. Although local and state governments and the professional machine tool association, the Association of Manufacturing Technology, are starting to provide support, it is not yet to the level of their foreign counterparts (Finegold et al., 1994, p.69).

Export controls have also weakened the export abilities of U.S. machine tool firms. The Coordinating Committee on Multilateral Export Controls was established by many Western nations to control the export of defense-related technologies to communist countries. The Committee was dissolved in March 1994, but much of their regulatory structure remains in order to control the export of these same technologies to hostile nations and the Third World.

Adding to these regulatory controls is the United States government's practice of further restricting exports through export administration acts. While the aforementioned regulatory environment restricted exports to certain parts of the world, export controls covered exports to anywhere in the world and were probably the largest hindrance to the export of American machine tools.

> The system set up to limit certain "high-tech" exports, including CNC machine tools, to specified countries indirectly deterred U.S. machine-tool exports by creating time-consuming, unpredictable export-licensing procedures (Finegold et al., 1994, p.71).

This process can take from six to nine months. Therefore, many firms will not even bother to apply for the licenses because they know by the time they receive it, their foreign competitors would have already received the business since it does not take them as long to get government approval (Finegold et al., 1994, p.70-71).

The lack of export finance has also made it difficult for U.S. machine tool firms to challenge their international competitors. Since Americans seek loans on the promise of repayment by foreign firms not covered by U.S. financial laws and regulations, banks consider it unacceptably risky to lend to machine tool firms for exports. Furthermore, the Export-Import Bank will guarantee loans for machine tool exports, but the sales are often too small to qualify for such guarantees. Thus, customers will buy their machine tools from producers in countries whose governments will guarantee the loans or offer a better deal.

As with many other goods, the American manufacturers argued that the large market share gained by these Japanese firms was due to the low value of the yen or to the dumping practices of the Japanese firms. While these factors may have played a role, probably the most significant reason for Japanese domination in this area is the underestimation by the American firms of the efficiency of the Japanese manufacturers and the reliability of their machine tools.

Evidence of this possibility is provided by the fact that the first of the Japanese numerically controlled machine tools were less expensive and more reliable than their American counterparts. Further evidence is provided by the extreme efficiency achieved by Fanuc.

By 1974 Fanuc had become the largest control builder in the world, measured by the number of controls produced, producing about 3,000 NC units a year with only 700 workers. This was at a time when the combined production of all the producers in the United States was about 4,000 units a year. Dr. Seiuemon Inaba, who had developed Fanuc from a department within the Japanese electric company Fuji Tsushinki, claimed that it would take any other NC producer with comparable sales about 3,000 workers to match Fanuc's volume (Ashburn, 1988, p.57).

Fanuc achieved such efficiency by having the complete production process under computer control and much of the production line mechanized. U.S. machine tool producers were slow to update their production processes and adopt new technologies, particularly CNC machines, which would have increased their productivity (more on this later). Therefore, it seems likely that the large market share gained by the Japanese was mainly due to the underestimation by the American manufacturers of the efficiency of the Japanese and of the reliability of their machines. Thus, one of the reasons for the slow adjustment of the American machine tool industry to international competition is the fact that they underestimated the strength of their competition.

The slow pace at which they reengineered their production processes is evident by their slow adoption of flexible manufacturing systems. These systems have become an important manufacturing technique because it provides many advantages to the manufacturer. For example, it allows the manufacturer to adjust quickly to changes in consumer demand and to offer more variety to customers. Furthermore, it reduces costs to some extent by lowering the amount of storage space by reducing the amount of finished goods that must be stored and by reducing set-up time and costs.

This technology has developed to the point at which flexible manufacturing cells can be operated unattended by a worker. While these unattended flexible manufacturing cells were readily adopted in Japan, the U.S. manufacturers were extremely hesitant to adopt them. One of the main reasons for this hesitancy was the specification in union contracts that there only be so many machines per worker. Obviously, this contractual barrier slowed the adoption of such flexible manufacturing cells since they required no workers.

It is possible, though, that this had an adverse effect on the ability of the American machine tool industry to adjust to foreign competition. After all, if there is no demand for these types of machines, the machine tool industry probably will not produce these machines or do research and development related to them. Thus, when U.S. manufacturers did finally begin to adopt this technology, the U.S. machine tool industry was forced to play catch-up to its Japanese counterparts.

The Role of Industry Structure

"For small firms operating in isolation, the array of new capacities and investments required for success in the current machine-tool marketplace is difficult to attain" (Finegold et al., 1994, p.32). Basically, the structure of the U.S. machine tool industry is such that it consists of "small firms operating in isolation." In order to compete in the machine tool marketplace of today, though, Finegold et al. (1994) recommend the industry either needs to establish: (1) some large firms that can achieve economies of scale and handle the requirements of new technologies and keep pace with technological advance or (2) a network among the small- to medium-sized companies that comprise the industry currently.

Before the demise of the U.S. industry, America contained the world's ten largest machine tool firms, but during the 1980s, this number dwindled to just one. "Japan now has nearly half of the world's largest machine-tool makers, and Germany has one-third, while the United States has only 8 percent" (Finegold et al., 1994, p.33). Although the American industry has restructured itself into a group of small firms, the industry can still be competitive by forming cooperative networks among the smaller firms, as their foreign counterparts have successfully done.

Unfortunately, this has not happened for a number of reasons. The U.S. industry is clustered (see chapter one), although not to the extent of some of its foreign rivals, but the cooperation among networks of firms does not exist.

> Among the reasons for this are antitrust regulation, which until recently prohibited any form of collusion; an unwillingness to share proprietary information; a lack of export orientation, which means firms tend to be vying for the same domestic customers; and a traditional American belief in the free market and independent entrepreneurs.... [Another] reason...has been a lack of an effective mechanism for setting and implementing technical standards,

which in turn inhibited the development of commodity CNC technology (Finegold et al., 1994, p.37).

This competition among the firms both inside and outside these clusters can be beneficial as it provides them with the impetus to be innovative (Porter, 1990). This has been the case in the industrial clusters of Japan and Germany, but the cooperative organizations have regulated the competition so that it is not just price-based. Thus, while competition exists in America's industry, given the structure of the machine tool industry, a little cooperation among the firms may have helped them maintain their leadership through the 1980s.

The Emergence of Conglomerates

While having an industry largely composed of small- to medium-sized firms hindered the industry's competitiveness, some of these firms were owned by large conglomerates. This was more detrimental than beneficial to their competitiveness, though. This was due to the fact that the conglomerates had a near-sighted investment horizon, which was compounded by the highly cyclical nature of the industry.

Being pushed by Wall Street to increase their earnings, the conglomerates used the high profits of the machine tool firms during an upturn in the business cycle to fund other ventures rather than reinvesting it in their machine tool branch. This push for immediate higher profits also caused them to focus on the manufacture of high-volume tools, since it was difficult to show a profit on the sale of specialized tools. This made the machine tool branch a manufacturer of a commodity, in essence, and thus, exposed the firm to the price competition and low profit margins that eventually comes with being in a commodity market.

The conglomerates had a similar disregard for the machine tool firm they owned during a downturn in the business cycle. Instead of investing in the firm to develop new products or upgrade its production systems, the conglomerates often simply sold off this part of their industrial portfolios, since it was no longer profitable. The owners of the firms did not understand the cyclical nature of the business, and with a short-term focus provided by Wall Street, the conglomerates often decided to just sell the machine tool firm. Thus, ownership of a machine tool firm by a conglomerate often spelled disaster for the machine tool firm, regardless of the state of the business cycle.

The Industry's Response to the Business Cycle

The machine tool industry's response to the business cycle only served to worsen its plight. During the upswing of the business cycle, the firms would backlog their orders so as to provide a cushion during the recession phase of the cycle. This meant delivery times of up to eighteen to twenty-four months. Such long delivery times opened the door for customers to buy the needed tools from foreign producers who could deliver the tools more quickly. Once they were then exposed to the service provided by the foreign manufacturers and the reliability of their tools, the customers often did not come back to the American firm. The other option left open to the machine tool users by the lengthy delivery times was to cancel the order altogether if the economy turned bad. Thus, while the conglomerate owners' responses to the business cycle did not help the cause of the American machine tool firm, their own response certainly did not help either.

The Myopic Vision of the Investment Community

The impact of an investment community with a short-term time horizon not only hurt the machine tool firms through their impact on the conglomerate who owned them, but it also had direct influences on the machine tool firms. Machine tool firms not owned by conglomerates were often times kept from making investments in costly machines because of the desire for profits to be derived from them within one to two years. Furthermore, the uncertainty of new technologies compounded these problems. If the company did make such investments, they exposed themselves to the corporate raiders so prevalent during the 1980s. The combination of these factors stifled the investments necessary for the industry to maintain its competitive abilities, facilitating the industry's demise.

A Shortage of Skilled Labor

As the technologies used by the machine tool industry have become more advanced, particularly with CNC, it has become increasingly important that the industry have a skilled pool of labor from which to draw employees. The United States has lacked a stock of skilled labor of the necessary magnitude for several reasons.

Much has been written and discussed about the importance of an educated labor force to the maintenance of a thriving economy. The U.S. machine tool industry provides a classic example of what can happen if the education "pipeline" fails. Relative to Germany and Japan, at least, the United States labor force is not as well educated in the basic skills - mathematics, science, and literacy - necessary for the machine tool industry to thrive.

After World War II, engineering schools shifted their curricula to a more science-based one that placed little emphasis on manufacturing. The departments were more interested in the more quantitative and scientific product design and analysis and thus, had a tendency to work more closely with the research and development and engineering departments of the companies (Dertouzos et al., 1989, p.240). They have not only shifted the emphasis of their curricula, but the universities are supplying fewer engineers with an interest in working in machine tools. "The U.S. machine-tool industry not only employs fewer engineers than the average for U.S. manufacturing, but it also has fewer engineers than Japan" (Finegold et al., 1994, p.46). Furthermore, more than half of those who have the title of "engineer" do not have a college degree (Finegold et al., 1994, p.46). Also, since the apprenticeship and occupational training programs are not as well developed as in many other nations, the vocational training of the labor force is not as extensive. "In sum, there is a relatively low supply of skills, at all levels, flowing from the U.S. education system into the machine-tool industry" (Finegold et al., 1994, p.47).

Having a workforce that is relatively poorly educated and lacking in the necessary basic skills has caused the industry to use less technologically advanced machines and to adapt CNC tools to the lower skill levels of their workers. Thus, they are not receiving the full productive benefits of the available advanced technologies.

One possible solution to this problem would be for companies to have in-house training for their employees. Unfortunately, disincentives impede such programs. A major disincentive is "poaching" of employees, once trained, by other firms. Given that layoffs often occur during a recession, the cyclical nature of the business cycle does not provide an incentive, either, to train the workers heavily, since many will be dismissed when the economy slows. Lastly, the skill levels of many of the workers are so poor that the firm may have to teach them basic literacy and math skills before they can even begin to teach them the necessary occupational skills. The upshot is that the education system has failed the industry but not much incentive exists for the industry to close the gap. The result is a pool of labor seriously lacking the necessary skills for the maintenance of a competitive industry.

A Lack of Significant Technological Progress

Forces from both the supply-side and demand-side hindered the rate of innovation and diffusion of technological advances in the machine tool industry. On the demand-side, a strong demand for more advanced technologies could have served to pull innovations out of the machine tool industry, but American manufacturers had grown overconfident of their competitive abilities. Thus, they saw little need to improve themselves, resulting in a lessened demand for new, state-of-the-art machine tools. Furthermore, increasing pressure from foreign competition combined with pressure from investors for short-term results caused many manufacturers to pursue cost-cutting measures. The companies slashed investment in new machines and increased price competition among suppliers, both of which provided significant disincentives to advance the state-of-the-art in machine tools.

In particular, these conditions provided barriers to the rapid adoption of a revolutionary development in machine tools - numerical control (NC) and computer numerical control (CNC). In comparison, the Japanese manufacturers adopted microprocessor-based controls four years before U.S. manufacturers did. Not only did they adopt the technology earlier; their machines based on microprocessor controls also proved to be more reliable.

Supply-side factors also played an important role in slowing the adoption of NC and CNC as well as the overall rate of technological advance in machine tools. Much of the federal research and development support focused on developing machine tools used to manufacture defense products led to the development of tools that were not particularly useful in private manufacturing or were too cost prohibitive. For example, numerically controlled tools were developed by the Servomechanisms Laboratory at MIT with financing provided by the U.S. Air Force. These tools were developed to be used to build complex parts used in the aircraft of the Air Force. Even though the Illinois Institute of Technology Research promoted diffusion of this technology, the technology was too costly for most private firms and was not readily adopted. Federal sponsorship of research at universities and laboratories also provided little benefit to the industry as "U.S. universities, with a few notable exceptions (e.g., Purdue, Lehigh), have neglected issues of manufacturing process in favor of product design and a more theoretical, science-based curriculum" (Finegold et al., 1994, p.41). Hence, the U.S. machine tool industry derived little benefit from federally-sponsored research and development.

Lastly, customers can be a good source of ideas for new technologies. By having open channels of communication with their customers, firms can learn their customers' needs and receive some guidance to their research and development. Close relationships with customers can also facilitate the implementation of the invention by receiving pertinent information and feedback from the customer regarding installation, proper design, and other characteristics of the equipment necessary to smoothly transition the tool from an invention to an innovation. Unfortunately, this type of relationship did not exist between U.S. machine tool firms and their customers. The lines of communication often were relatively poor and few strategic alliances or partnerships existed between manufacturer and client in which financing of the necessary R&D was shared. The result of this combination of the aforementioned conditions was an industry mired in old technologies being passed by its more innovative foreign competitors.

The Failure of Government Policies and Regulations

The policies and regulations implemented by the different levels of government have done little to assist the nation's machine tool industry. Some examples follow.

The financial regulations imposed on banks by both federal and state governments have increased the cost of capital by increasing both the documentation required in loan applications and the cost of processing the application. This has had the effect of making much financial capital unavailable to many of the smaller machine tool firms.

The uncertainty of changes in the tax laws has also slowed investment as uncertainty about the economic future is increased.

The product liability system has also been a hindrance to the development of the industry as the firms have been forced to defend themselves against an increasing number of lawsuits (both legitimate and ludicrous). It has increased costs to the point "that, on average, machine-tool firms spend up to seven times more on [liability] insurance premiums than on R&D" (Finegold et al., 1994, p.59). This is not to say that the liability laws had the same effects as a poorly educated labor force. They probably did not, but since it is hard to measure the differential impacts of liability laws, it is difficult to say for sure. Besides, the foreign firms might have to endure stiffer regulations in other areas that impose higher costs than those imposed on U.S. firms.

Difilippo (1986) has argued that too much defense spending has also hurt the machine tool industry. He presents a three-pronged argument. First, defense spending has crowded-out federal support for commercially-oriented machine tool industry research and development. Second, placing so much emphasis on defense has led to a conflict of interest between the defense establishment and the machine tool industry causing many machine tool exports to be stopped in the name of national security. Third, the sporadic nature of defense spending heightened the sensitivity of the industry to the business cycle as machine tool firms were uncertain as to whether or not they could count on the support of such spending during bad times. Such uncertainty did not provide incentives to expand R&D spending within the industry.

As often occurs when an industry is experiencing rough economic times in international markets, there have been numerous cries for an industrial policy providing protection and support to the machine tool industry by the federal government. Recent events, though, have proven these pundits wrong as the industry has started to turn itself around without the assistance of an industrial policy.

Recent Rebirth of the Industry[2]

The good news in this story is that the industry was finally able to make an adequate number of adjustments, combined with help from both domestic and international markets and slight assistance from the federal government, to mount a comeback within the past decade. Domestically, demand for machine tools expanded, led by the U.S. automakers. The Big Three increased their demand for machine tools by 81% between 1992 and 1994, and a sizeable portion of these orders went to U.S. suppliers.

---

2 This discussion is drawn largely from Robinson (1996).

In the international arena, U.S. toolmakers expanded their exports from 16% of production in 1984 to 35% in 1995. The rising Yen and increased export support from the federal government facilitated this. For example, the U.S. Department of Commerce helped the machine tool trade association establish a field office in Beijing in 1993.

Further assistance from the federal government came in the form of voluntary restraint agreements (VRA's) imposed in 1987 on six classes of machine tools from Taiwan and Japan. They expired in 1993, but the protection gave the U.S. industry enough time to regroup to the point of increasing research and development spending from five percent of sales in 1987 to twelve percent of sales in 1992.

The increased research and development surely helped the industry's rate of innovation, but also facilitating this process was the fact that machine tool firms began to form relationships with their customers. Instead of telling the customer what they needed, the supplier would actually seek to understand the customer's needs and develop new tools accordingly. They would also work with the customer during the design phase of the innovative process, which helped the machine tool firm create new tools desired by their clients that readily fit into their production process.

The industry would not have been able to regain some of their lost market share if they had not improved the quality of their tools and the service that accompanied them. U.S. machine tools are now considered to be of equal quality to those made by German and Japanese firms. Not only have they matched the Japanese and Germans on quality, but the U.S. firms are also shipping their machines in as timely a manner accompanied with equivalent service and technical support.

The U.S. machine tool industry faced some formidable barricades to their success, but they have slowly begun to respond to the challenge and remove some of those barricades. The result is turning out to be an industry that is more innovative and able to compete in an increasingly international machine tool market. Evidence of this is provided by the $4.8 billion in orders they received in 1995. This is twice the amount of orders they received in 1992 and the largest since the late 1970s when they were leaders of the market. This does not mean that they have regained their leadership status, though. The U.S. industry is still behind Germany and Japan, regaining the third spot from Italy. The ability to create new machine tools at a rapid pace will be a key element in their future success and will surely play some role in their push to once again become the worldwide leader in machine tool production. The factors that influence the efficiency with which the industry produces machine tool invention patents - a first step in the innovative process - is the concern of this study. Hopefully, then, this study will further our understanding of the indigenous potential within the economy that helped the industry pull itself out of its dire circumstances of the recent past and that will facilitate the invention - and thus, the innovation - necessary to enhance the competitiveness of the U.S. machine tool industry in the future.

A Classic Case of Creative Destruction

Facing numerous obstacles to its survival, the decade of the 1980s appeared to be one of considerable crisis for the U.S. machine tool industry. It appeared that this tumultuous era was leading the industry to its ultimate demise, but it was able to withstand the "destruction" and restructure itself into a form better able to compete in today's economy. In contrast to the appearances, this was not an era of crisis leading to the extinction of the U.S. machine tool industry, but rather, it was a time of Schumpeterian creative destruction, such as also occurred in the 1820s, the 1870s, and the 1920s (Berry, 1991).

The result of part of the restructuring process was to improve the inventive and innovative abilities of the industry. Enhancing these abilities played a significant role in the eventual return to prominence of the industry.

3 What Stimulates Invention? A Review of the Literature

The Case for Demand-Pull

In his classic work, *Invention and Economic Growth*, Jacob Schmookler analyzes the stimuli for invention patents. His analysis begins with an examination of the effect of knowledge on patenting activity. In particular, he proposes two hypotheses: "(1) important inventions are typically induced by scientific discoveries [and] (2) inventions are typically induced by the intellectual stimuli provided by earlier inventions" (Schmookler, 1966, pp.57-58). As a test of his first hypothesis, the economically and/or technologically important inventions from four industries - petroleum refining, paper making, railroading, and farming - were chosen. The relevant literatures were searched for suggestions that a scientific discovery led to an important invention. For almost all those inventions in which a stimulus is given, the

> stimulus *is a technical problem or opportunity conceived by the inventor largely in economic terms* [emphasis Schmookler's]....*In no single instance is a scientific discovery specified as the factor initiating an important invention in any of these four industries* [emphasis mine] (Schmookler, 1966, pp.66-67).

Therefore, Schmookler concluded that technical advance is at least as much an economic phenomenon as it is a technological one.

Schmookler contended that these results would hold in other industries like the electrical, electronics, nuclear, chemical, drug, and pharmaceutical industries. Even though the electrical, electronics, and nuclear industries are heavily dependent on science, he argued the conclusion would still stand with only slight modifications.

There are three reasons for this. First, the dominant catalyst of inventive activity is still economically valuable technical problems and opportunities. Second, even if important inventions arose out of scientific discoveries, their social and economic importance are the result of improving and adapting the shortcomings of the basic invention and seizing the economic opportunities the invention creates. "Thus, the important inventions in a field which follow the basic one are likely to arise from the exposure of creative minds to technical-economic phenomena" (Schmookler, 1966, p.69). Third, even if the idea for an invention resulted from a scientific discovery, the decision to proceed with an invention is an investment decision.

These results led Schmookler to conclude that the roles of science in the process of technical change are to further the knowledge of inventors, allowing them to envision inventions unimaginable by their predecessors. In other words, "vital though it is, *scientific discovery is far more a permissive than an active factor in the inventive process*" [emphasis mine] (Schmookler, 1966, p.70). Thus, according to Schmookler, invention is not, in large part, stimulated by scientific discovery.

In his analysis of the second hypothesis, the evidence did not lend support to the idea that invention is facilitated by the knowledge and intellectual stimulus of past inventions. As Schmookler argues,

> the point here is simply that since inventions, important and otherwise, generally represent creative responses to felt wants, the means for satisfying these wants in some measure are usually found through one channel if not through another; so that, if a particular important invention had never appeared on the scene, something approximating a functionally equivalent invention would probably have been made and used, or taken off the shelf if it had already been made (Schmookler, 1966, p.136).

In short, it is the demand for a certain invention, not the intellectual stimulus of a previous invention, that stimulates inventors.

A third hypothesis considered by Schmookler is that the decline of inventive activity within an industry may be due to "the exhaustion of the field's technical possibilities" (Schmookler, 1966, p.87). The idea here is that an industry may be born out of some scientific discovery or a major invention may be created within the industry which will subsequently initiate a sequence of inventions that make improvements or adjustments to the major invention or discovery. Eventually, though, there will be less upon which to improve and the inventive potential of the industry will begin to decline. Schmookler analyzed this issue in terms of productivity - defining the technological novelty of an invention in terms of changes in productivity. In this light, as technological advance reaches its limit within an industry, "improvements in physical productivity become increasingly difficult and therefore costly" (Schmookler, 1966, p.89). Thus, the question becomes: Is the decline of inventive activity within an industry due to the rising cost of a given percentage increase in productivity (i.e. technological advance), or is it due to the decrease in value of the technological advance? Put yet another way, is the initial rise and then subsequent decline in inventive activity over the long term the result of the interaction between the rising value of productivity advance and the rising cost of productivity advance with the decline being the result of rising costs eventually overtaking the rising value? Or, is it that the industry never even reaches its technological limits, so that the rise and fall of inventive activity is due to the rise and fall in the value of advances in productivity, respectively?

To begin his search for an answer, Schmookler analyzed the case of the horseshoe, and he found that the decline in horseshoe patents corresponded with the replacement of the horse with the steam traction and combustion engines. Thus, the decline in horseshoe-related inventive activity correlated with a decline in the economic value of such inventions, not the decline in the technical possibilities.

Probing further, he examined the patenting cycles of two industrially complementary technologies (i.e. both are used in production of the same good) - track and nontrack railroad inventions. The cycles were extremely similar to each other, indicating that changes in the cycles were due to economic forces. Since they are complementary, increases in the value of a productivity advance in one should also increase the value of an advance in the complementary technology. On the other hand, since each is a separate technology, changes in the costs of a certain magnitude of productivity advance would be different between the two fields. Thus, if the cycles of patenting activity were driven by the costs of technological advance, there would be no necessary similarities in the cycles.

The evidence does not prove that changes in inventive activity are driven by responses to changes in the value of productivity advance. Still further evidence in support of the idea that the value of invention, not costs, is what drives inventive activity was found in a comparison of the patent cycles of railroad, building, and "all other" (included chemicals, electricity, electronics, and instruments) industries. The similarity in these cycles indicated that the inventive activity in the building industry and the "all other" category of industries was influenced by the value of invention, as was the case in the railroad industry. After all, if intellectual stimuli, the cost of invention, or the intraindustry rate of diffusion were the main driving force, such similarities in their patenting cycles would not be expected. These results allowed Schmookler to reach the conclusion

> that *taken as a whole* the movement of American inventive activity in all fields responded more to common external factors, presumably economic circumstances affecting mainly the value of productivity advances, than to either intellectual stimuli, changes in the expected costs of those advances, or intra-industry diffusion patterns (Schmookler, 1966, p.101).

In other words, the main engine propelling invention comes from the demand-side rather than the supply-side.

The results were similar in his analysis of the relationship between investment in capital goods and capital goods invention. Using both cross-sectional and time-series data for the railroad, building, and petroleum refining industries, Schmookler found support for his theory that the level of capital goods invention varies directly with the expected size of the market. In other words, the causal order between investment and invention is that investment in capital goods causes capital goods invention, not vice versa. In particular, "*a 1 percent increase in investment tends to induce a 1 percent increase in capital goods invention*" (Schmookler, 1966, p.144).

Thus, in all the possible relationships considered, the main catalyst for invention was "the wants of men." It is the expected economic value (i.e. the extent of the market) of an invention, not intellectual stimuli or the limits of technological possibilities, that is the main determinant of inventive activity.

This is not to say that Schmookler believed supply-side considerations completely lacked importance. Science and technology are important in that they permit the creation of certain inventions, and thus the body of knowledge will influence the characteristics of an invention. Put another way, the body of scientific knowledge will influence the scientific realms from which the inventor draws to create the invention, but it does not provide the impetus for undertaking the invention in the first place.

Another reason that supply-side considerations are of secondary importance is that "mankind today possesses, and for some time has possessed, a multi-purpose knowledge base. We are, and evidently for some time have been, able to extend the technological frontier perceptibly at virtually all points" (Schmookler, 1966, p.210). The upshot of this is that the upper limit on invention is too far ahead of the frontier to influence inventive effort. Hence, supply-side considerations do exert some influence on inventive activity, but ultimately it is "demand [that] induces the inventions that satisfy it" (Schmookler, 1966, p.184).

The Case for Supply-Push

Rosenberg (1974) disagrees with the notion that supply-side factors are secondary to those of the demand-side. That is, he disagrees with Schmookler's idea that the scientific and technical knowledge base exerts only permissive influences on inventive activity. He also disagrees with the idea that there are virtually no limits placed on invention in any industry since mankind's scientific and technical knowledge is "multi-purpose and can be expanded at will. From Rosenberg's point of view, "...knowledge not only permits-it also constrains" (Rosenberg, 1974, p.106).

Obviously, Rosenberg believes supply-side forces play a role that is at least as significant as demand-side forces in shaping the direction and level of inventive activity.

> In fact, ..., if we want to explain the historical sequence in which different categories of want have been satisfied *via* the inventive process, we must pay attention to a special supply side variable: the growing stock of useful knowledge. Historical evidence confirms that inventions are rarely equally possible in all commodity classes. The state of the various sciences simply make some inventions easier (i.e., cheaper) and others harder (i.e., more costly). In considering the manner in which the stock of scientific knowledge has grown, and the manner in which this growth has, in turn, shaped the possibilities for inventive activity, one basic fact stands out: The world of nature contains many sub-realms, which vary enormously in their relative complexity (Rosenberg, 1974, p.98).

In other words, there is a direct relationship between invention and both the state of scientific knowledge and the complexity of the technology necessary to carry out research in the field.

For example, consider the case of medicine. Certainly there has always been a significant demand for advances in medicine, but it was not until progress in bacteriology was made that significant gains in the treatment of infectious diseases were made. Or with respect to the influence of the complexity of necessary technologies, consider the case of diabetes in which progress in the treatment of this disease was stifled until the creation of X-ray crystallography allowed the deciphering of the extremely complex insulin molecule.

In response to Schmookler's argument that sub-realms of knowledge offer substitutes for ways to devise inventions in order to satisfy demand, Rosenberg argues that this is not always the case. "Such substitution is frequently non-existent and usually highly imperfect. Moreover, in many cases the inventive process confronts relationships of complementarity rather than substitution" (Rosenberg, 1974, p.100). For example, the creation of hybrid foods such as rice and corn that are higher-yield crops are not actually more "productive" unless combined with large increases in fertilizer and pesticides. That is, advances in biology have allowed scientists to create a strain of rice, for example, that is more productive, but it has to be combined with chemicals such as fertilizer and pesticides in order to attain the higher yields.

Rosenberg also argues that invention and the adoption of technological advances depends on the nature of the technical problems created by the adoption of a particular technology and the ability of those in the industry to overcome the problems. Hence, even though rising relative prices of firewood in Great Britain provided a strong economic impetus to substitute coal for wood, it took many industries two hundred years to make the substitution. Those industries that faced few problems in making the substitution made the switch to coal quickly, while others faced substantial problems when making the switch to coal and thus, took much longer in making the substitution. In fact, the order in which different industries solved the problems of substituting coal for wood depended on the technical difficulties faced by the industry, even though all faced significant economic payoffs to make the switch. Thus, although demand-side factors provided a stimulus for switching to coal, the inventions needed to make the switch possible came at various times across industries, depending on the severity of the technical problems that the invention was trying to solve. It seems, as Rosenberg argues, that supply-side forces are a strong determinant of both an invention's probability of success within a particular period of time and the cost to produce a successful invention. In other words, "given the state of purely scientific knowledge, society's technical competence at any point in time constitutes a basic determinant of the kinds of inventions which can be successfully undertaken" (Rosenberg, 1974, p.105).

According to the arguments of Schmookler and Rosenberg, then, technological change is influenced by both demand-side and supply-side considerations. Conceptualizing technological change in terms of these general demand-side and supply-side influences frames the subject broadly. But, just as the details of a painting lie inside its frame, we want to focus inside this broad frame of demand and supply to the details of what specific factors drive technological change. In particular, we want to look at the factors that stimulate the first step of technological change – invention. The next section will chronicle some of these factors.

Stimulants to Inventive Activity

The literature on inventive factors is substantial and diverse, but six principal stimulants appear to dominate discussion: (1) agglomeration economies, (2) human capital, (3) producer services, (4) investment in information technology, (5) federal funding, and (5) invention-derived knowledge.

Agglomeration Economies

Agglomeration economies defined Agglomeration economies are external economies of scale realized by the firm due to the scale of economic activity occurring within its economic surroundings. As defined by Kaldor (1970), agglomeration economies are

> nothing else but the existence of increasing returns to scale - using that term in the broadest sense - in processing activities. These are not just the economies of large-scale production, commonly considered, but the cumulative advantages accruing from the growth of industry itself - the development of skill and know-how; the opportunities for easy communication of ideas and experience, the opportunity of ever-increasing differentiation of processes and of specialization in human activities (Kaldor, 1970, p.340).

Agglomeration economies not only register their effects on urban centers but also on the areas surrounding the urban center (Pred, 1966; von Boventer, 1970), which provides, in part, an argument for using metro-regions as the geographic unit of interest.

Localization economies   Economists have recognized two forms of agglomeration economies - *localization* economies and *urbanization* economies.   A firm realizes localization economies from the size of the firm's industry within a region (Carlino, 1979;   Shefer, 1973).   The firm realizes gains in productivity through several mechanisms.   Localized agglomerations make it viable for the development of firms that serve particular needs of the industry.   Firms gain access to these services at a lower cost than maintaining in-house services or contracting for the necessary services from afar.   These clusters of firms produce clusters of workers who can readily move from one firm to another.   This means there is not only a suitable supply of labor, but the interactions of these workers spawns and transfers ideas that facilitate technological change (Carlino, 1987; *The Economist*, 29 March 1997).

Urbanization economies   Urbanization economies arise out of the size of a region.   In particular, they depend on the number of business enterprises within a region.   For example, larger urban areas tend to have the public infrastructures (e.g. roads and educational facilities) to support innovation (Carlino, 1993; Carlino and Voith, 1992; Suarez-Villa and Hasnath, 1993). An agglomeration of firms of various sorts allows other firms to achieve economies of scale via access to a diversity of specialized services.   Firms in large urban areas not only have ready access to banks, advertising agencies, wholesalers, law firms, and others, but exceptionally large regions have firms that specialize in different areas of banking and advertising.   Firms in small areas cannot achieve the advantages these firms provide because they do not have easy access (Carlino, 1987).[1]

Agglomeration economies and technological change   It is through "the development of skill and know-how" and "the opportunities for easy communication of ideas and experience" that agglomeration economies accelerate the rate of technological change.   Jacobs (1969) and Pred (1966) suggest that large cities play a key role in the development of new

---

[1] For empirical evidence of the existence of urbanization economies, see studies by Carlino (1979), Kawashima (1975), Segal (1976) and Sveikauskas (1975).

technologies. This is due to the disproportionately large number of skilled workers, researchers, and entrepreneurs willing to invest in technological change located in these regions. These regions facilitate the interaction of these players, which facilitates the flow of ideas and the rate of technical change.

The agglomeration of firms within a region increases the number and facilitates the flow of signals and information about the profitability of new technologies across the firms. As Beeson (1987) shows, a density of economic activity can increase the rate of technical change through this mechanism. Hagerstrand (1967) also argues for the importance of communication in the diffusion of innovations.

The diffusion of new technologies through regions is generally thought to follow two patterns. In a pattern of hierarchical diffusion, innovation begins in the largest regions and then is transmitted through the hierarchy of regions to the smaller ones (Berry, 1972; Griliches, 1957; Mansfield, 1968; Pederson, 1970). The second pattern (Morrill, 1968) - radial diffusion - "is characterized by an inverse relationship between distance from the source of the innovation and the time it takes for the innovation to reach an area" (Beeson, 1987, p.186).

No matter what the pattern of the diffusion of innovations is, the key point is that agglomeration economies are a catalyst to the diffusion process. Agglomeration economies are important for innovation diffusion since agglomeration economies for people attract the innovating elite while agglomeration economies for businesses attract the firms, research and development institutions and other corporations that may increase a region's capacity to absorb innovations (Richardson, 1973).

Thus, by acting as facilitator, it is not much of a leap of faith to expect that agglomeration economies will increase the flow of relevant information via feedback from those who have adopted an innovation. It is these feedback flows that help drive further technological change (Kline and Rosenberg, 1986).

Human Capital

The role of human capital in the production of goods and services is well documented. As Acs and Audretsch (1988, 1989), Feldman (1992), Griliches (1979), Jaffe (1986, 1989), and Mansfield (1981) have shown, the production of patents or innovations can be observed in a similar light as the production of "standard" goods and services using a production function approach. The production function for patents, as in most any production function, has as two of its major inputs physical capital and labor or human capital.

Suarez-Villa has done considerable work showing the role of various institutional mechanisms in developing regional *innovative capacity* (a concept similar to innovation potential). One of the most important mechanisms, in his opinion, are those supporting the development of human capital (Suarez-Villa, 1993; Suarez-Villa and Hasnath, 1993). In fact, he argues that "the development of major loci of invention may reflect a higher quantitative level of human capital resources and infrastructure..." (Suarez-Villa, 1993, p.148). Thus, supporting a region's expression of its inventive prowess is a significant stock of qualified human capital (Allison et al. 1982; Bartel and Lichtenberg 1987; Wozniak 1987).

In a series of papers, Acs and Audretsch (1987, 1988, 1989) measure, among other inputs, the importance of skilled labor as an input in the production of innovations. Using a log-linear production function approach, they show that skilled labor plays a key role in the production process of innovations, especially in small firms. Furthermore, they find support for their hypothesis that small firms are more innovative in the early stages of the product cycle since the production process is fairly labor intensive and a high level of skilled labor is required to adjust for the rapid changes in product design. This is support for the notion that regions with a significant stock of skilled labor are better suited to develop their innovation potential since the labor force is equipped to easily adapt to technological change allowing the firm to achieve some reasonable return from their innovations.

Their 1989 paper "Patents as a Measure of Innovative Activity" is an extension of their 1987 and 1988 papers. The purpose of this study was "to compare whether the patent measure performs similarly to the direct measure of innovative activity" (Acs and Audretsch, 1989, p.173). In order to do the comparison, they used the same production-function model, the only change being in the dependent variable, which was defined as the total number of patented inventions. All of the independent variables remained the same.

The regression results indicated that with the exception of some of the appropriability measures, all of the relationships (i.e., measures of knowledge and firm size) were the same for both total patents and innovative activity. Of the four appropriability measures used - market concentration, advertising

38

intensity, capital intensity, and unionization – only market concentration and advertising intensity showed similar effects. Thus, the patent measure did perform similarly to the direct measure of innovation. Specifically, skilled labor was still found to be a significant contributor to patenting activity. Skilled labor, therefore, appears to be an important input in the production of innovations or patents (i.e. innovation potential) for a couple of reasons. First, it is necessary to have skilled labor in the form of scientists, engineers, and others engaged in the innovative process. Second, having a stock of skilled labor within a localized economy gives firms the ability to adopt innovations because they know their labor force will be able to adapt. This provides a firm with an incentive to engage in R&D and the production of innovations.

University presence: Training and knowledge creation   It is commonly thought that the regions like San Jose, California (i.e. Silicon Valley), Boston, Massachusetts around Route 128, Austin, Texas, and Raleigh/Durham, North Carolina have become leading centers of technological change because of their proximity to major universities (Dorfman, 1983; Jaffe, 1989). As Jaffe (1989) states,

> It is certainly plausible that the pool of talented graduates, the ideas generated by faculty, and the high quality libraries and other facilities of research universities facilitate the process of commercial innovation in their neighborhood (Jaffe, 1989, p.957).

Stated within the context of this study, it seems plausible that universities can facilitate the development of regional innovation potential through several channels.

For example, Nelson (1982) argues that university research produces knowledge which focuses R&D activities on the subset of projects that will lower the cost of achieving a certain advance or increase the magnitude of the advance given a certain R&D outlay. In other words, university research improves the productivity of corporate R&D.[2] In his 1986 work, Nelson

---

[2] Extending this argument, Nelson makes an interesting point regarding the Schmookler-Rosenberg debate discussed earlier. He argues that finding the optimum strategy does not necessarily mean more input. "The result may be regarded as a special case of a general proposition in price theory: an increase in the productivity of an input leads to greater output in the optimum solution but not necessarily more input" (Nelson, 1982, p.459). This line of thought may actually resolve at least part of the debate between Schmookler and Rosenberg.

reiterated this position, and from these more recent findings, he added two more important roles: universities are important as training grounds for scientists engaged in R&D, and university research increases the technological opportunities available to an industry.

Universities also keep the region and its industrial researchers at the cutting edge of technology (Dosi, 1988; Nelson, 1996; Rosenberg and Nelson, 1994).

> Universities emphasize the free exchange and flow of information: their existence in an area creates an intellectual commons with the implied spill-overs of knowledge. In contrast to the common notion that knowledge is a public good easily transferred via publications, gaining commercial control over a new technology requires access to those knowledgeable with the technology (Feldman, 1992, pp.23-24).

Grefsheim et al. (1991) show how important these face-to-face interactions are in a survey of biotechnology researchers. They found these interactions to be vital because they provided information in a more timely manner, before printed sources became available, and because the interactions allowed the researchers to more accurately and fully express their thoughts on the impacts of their work, their methods, and their results. Nelson (1996) reports that the results of a survey of industrial R&D managers indicate that these managers find university research in mechanical engineering relevant to the development of hand tools and specialized machinery technology. These R&D managers also believe university research in electrical engineering is valuable to the development of semiconductor technology. The upshot is that

> It appears that university research causes industry R&D and not vice versa. Thus, a state [or region] that improves its university research system will increase local innovation both by attracting industrial R&D and augmenting its productivity (Jaffe, 1989, p.968).

It should be noted that this proposition puts a different light on the apparent difference between Rosenberg and Schmookler regarding the role of basic knowledge in R&D allocation. There may be no conflict at all. Stronger knowledge within this model, at least, is associated with more rapid progress – Rosenberg's point. However, there is no reason to expect any systematic connection between the strength of the knowledge base and the total amount of R&D input being applied – Schmookler's proposition (Nelson 1982, 459-460).

Feldman (1992) and Mansfield (1991) confirm Jaffe's conclusion.

In a broader sense, Suarez-Villa and Hasnath (1993) found support for this argument. They analyzed the effect of educational infrastructure investment on corporate and aggregate innovative capacity (defined as the total number of patents granted in the region over a seventeen-year period). While their definition of educational infrastructure investment covers education at all levels and thus, is broader than just investment in universities, they still find a positive role for the educational infrastructure in the innovative process. Particularly, their analysis led them to conclude that educational infrastructure investment influences both aggregate and corporate innovative capacity with a lag.

Nelson (1986) argued that universities improve the prospects for technological change in a region (i.e. enhance the innovation potential) by conducting research that both increases technological opportunities and improves the productivity of industrial R&D. To summarize, universities provide a vital function in the production of the innovation potential of a region because they lower the cost of attaining the information needed by firms, researchers, inventors, and others involved in the inventive process (Davelaar and Nijkamp, 1989).

Producer Services

The processes of invention and innovation are complex ones, and thus, information can play a vital role in this process. One source of such information is the various firms in the producer or business services industry. Similar to the role of universities, these firms provide information of various sorts that can catalyze the inventive process (Davelaar and Nijkamp, 1989). For example, market research firms provide information about the level of demand for certain products in the market; attorneys help the inventors through the patenting process; and commercial testing labs assure the new product meets specifications (Berry, Conkling, and Ray, 1987; Coffey and Polese, 1987; Feldman, 1992; Florida and Kenney, 1990; MacPherson, 1991).

Providing such services within the confines of a firm is generally beyond the reach of all but the largest of firms. Thus, it is important for firms interested in innovation to locate within regions that have a sound

41

producer services industry (empirical evidence of this is provided by many of the works cited above). Otherwise, they will have to attain such services across great distances or find a way to provide the services themselves. Either way, the result is an increase in the costs of attaining these services relative to being located within a region with an adequate base of producer services suppliers (Davelaar and Nijkamp, 1989). Fortunately, producer services firms have a tendency to locate near those to whom they are supplying information (Coffey and Polese, 1987). The reverse is also true. Because of the value of the information provided by the producer services firms, firms using this information are strongly attracted to areas with a base of producer services specializing in their industry (Florida and Kenney, 1990). The cluster of producer services firms creates a self-reinforcing process of positive feedback that attracts other firms to the region resulting in industrial concentrations within the region (Arthur, 1990).

Information Technology Investment

Information and the transfer of that information are vital inputs to the inventive and innovative process. One of the key roles universities play in this process is as disseminator of important technical information in a timely manner through face-to-face interaction. Another transfer mechanism is the multi-user computer network (hereafter called information technology or IT) (Grefsheim et al., 1991).

Investment in IT infrastructure can facilitate the development of a region's innovation potential in two ways. First, investment in such technologies generally represents "the investments of major corporate-scale enterprise at production, service, R&D, and administrative sites" (Hicks and Nivin, 1995, p.14). To the extent that these investments flow to centers of research and development, such an explanatory variable will capture the presence of these centers. Furthermore, IT investment should improve the quality and efficiency of the R&D, which should, in turn, improve the region's innovation potential.

Second, "information plays a large role in the process of innovation – information that is not sought or available to competitors, or information available to others that is interpreted in new ways" (Porter, 1990, p.48). Information can give the inventors new ideas or provide them with the technical information that solves a problem (Mansfield, 1968; Myers and

Marquis, 1969; Rosenberg, 1982). Given the uncertainty of the process of technological change, having access to vital information is very important.

> This uncertainty, by which we mean an inability to predict the outcome of the search process, or to predetermine the most efficient path to some particular goal, has a very important implication: the activity cannot be planned....Vital information will become available at some future point which cannot, in the nature of the case, be made available now. It would be folly to lock oneself into a predetermined pattern of behavior, because this amounts to depriving oneself of the benefit of additional information, of a kind that may be decisive to success or failure, that can only become available in the future (Rosenberg, 1994, p.93).

For these reasons, investment in a technology that facilitates the flow of information, as multi-user network information technology does, should positively influence the development of the innovation potential of a region.

Federally Funded Research and Development

Federal R&D spending has been shown to register an impact on local incomes and employment (Hicks and Lee, 1994; Malecki, 1984; Mehay and Skolnick, 1990). These developmental effects of federally-funded R&D

> could indicate a chain of economic events whereby federal R&D flows stimulate increased regional capacities to incubate and host new rounds of technical innovation and business formation/expansion that eventually come to be registered on indicators of overall regional economic performance (Hicks and Lee, 1994).

The incubating and hosting of new rounds of innovation spawned by flows of federally funded R&D can be interpreted to mean that such flows may enhance the innovation potential of the region. Most earlier studies have been interested in how federal flows of R&D express themselves in the development of regional economies. This study is interested in one step prior to this expression, however. As Hicks and Lee (1994) stated, federal R&D funding may facilitate the development of regional innovation potential which may, in turn, have an impact on the economic development of the region. Does federally funded R&D, in fact, facilitate the development of metro-regional innovation potential?

43

Scherer (1983) found that industries whose R&D are federally funded will have a lower propensity to patent. This is due to the fact that the government insisted on having title or a license that is royalty-free on any invention supported by federal funds. However, in part because federal R&D financing enhances the potential of company-financed R&D to produce invention patents, he found a positive relationship between the patenting of firms within particular industries and federal R&D support, providing evidence that R&D supported federal monies may, in fact, facilitate the development of a region's innovation potential.

Invention-Derived Knowledge

Beggs (1984) analyzed the effects that past inventions have on future inventions. He found that past invention patents influenced inventive activity with lags of five and eight years. The initial five- year lag is due to the time it takes "to understand and develop the original patent and to then understand and produce the appropriate follow-up invention" (Beggs, 1984, p.164). This five-year lag is followed by another lag of three years in which the inventors produce follow-up patents based on the work done in the initial five-year period. This second lag is shorter than the first because of the knowledge and experience gained with the new technology.

A further interesting point Beggs made concerns the transmission process of follow-up inventions across industries. In particular, he states:

> Since these are national aggregate patents, one might expect longer lags than if one simply studied a patent series within a single industry. Inventions in one industry may lead to follow-up inventions in other industries, but the transmission process will be slower. For example, a patent issued for a semiconductor invention may be associated with a rapid follow-up patent in semiconductors, but the follow-up patent in, say, automated tool cutting will occur much later (Beggs, 1984, pp.164-165).

In what follows, I seek to provide more evidence on the time lags in the transmission process of follow-up inventions from semiconductors to machine tools and from within the machine tool industry itself.

Demand-pull: More evidence As indicated earlier, Schmookler was interested in the relationships between both investment and invention and past inventions and present invention. Along similar lines, Beggs (1984) ran a series of two variable regressions analyzing the linkages between patents and investment, competition, wages, and previous patents. All variables were rates of change and were measured relative to the national aggregate where relevant. Measuring the variables relative to the national aggregates removed the effect of the business cycle on movements in the variables.

He found evidence that investment had a demand-pull effect on patents which means "that many new inventions are embodied in new capital equipment" (Beggs, 1984, p.161). He also found that "in periods of severe competitive pressure, brought on by the encroachment of other industries onto its turf, firms may respond by quickening the tempo of their inventive efforts" (Beggs, 1984, p.162) as the firms search for more competitive production processes and products. There thus exists a direct relationship between a firm's patenting activity and the degree of competition the firm faces. Finally, Beggs found no linkage between patents and wages. There was no evidence that movements in wages in an industry relative to the national average was a function of the nature of technological change in that industry. Wages were apparently not influenced by technological changes that lowered or raised the skill requirements of the labor force or by the ability of labor in strongly unionized industries to extract some of the economic rents resulting from technological change. Other researchers, though, have found a significant relationship between increased skill requirements resulting from technological change and wage gains. For instance, Hicks and Nivin (1995) found that increased requirements of computer competence in the local labor force accompanied wage gains during the 1980s.

Regional Economies and Inventive Performance

Much of the stimulus for this dissertation came from Luis Suarez-Villa's April 1993 work, "The Dynamics of Regional Invention and Innovation: Innovative Capacity and Regional Change in the Twentieth Century." Suarez-Villa developed a measure of inventive output that he called *innovative capacity*, defining it as "the aggregate stock of invention patents that are legally available for application" (Suarez-Villa, 1993, p.149). The measure was calculated for four multi-state regions - Rustbelt, Northeast, Midwest, and Sunbelt - by summing all patents granted in each region over periods of seventeen years.

45

Using graphical analysis, he showed that the Northeast retained a dominant role as a locus of invention from 1900-1940, and while the Midwest maintained a less dominant role than the Northeast throughout the twentieth century, its invention patent behavior paralleled the behavior of the Northeast. As a locus of invention, the Sunbelt was a minor one relative to the Northeast and Midwest, but the Sunbelt's patent performance during the postwar era allowed it to overtake both the Northeast and Midwest as the main locus for invention patents.

Suarez-Villa offered several reasons for this reversal of roles. He argued that the long-term shift to a services-based economy and the movement of the population toward the Sunbelt states were key to this region's ability to enhance its innovative capacity. The shift also

> reflected the economic emergence of this region. Key Sunbelt states, such as California, Texas, and Florida attracted inventors and research-intensive firms from the heartland regions, promoted the creation of major technology corporations, and developed substantial research poles in various locations (Suarez-Villa, 1993, p.155).

The shift to a services economy resulting in both population and employment growth, infrastructural development, and the economic emergence of the Sunbelt all played a significant part in the reversal of regional roles in regards to innovative capacity.

To further support the evidence of the rising importance of the Sunbelt as a locus of invention patents, Suarez-Villa developed another indicator - patent age cycles - which was related to innovative capacity. "Age cycles are defined as the changing distribution of patent age segments over their legal life term of seventeen years" (Suarez-Villa, 1993, p.155). He divided the patents into three age groups: 0-5 years, 6-11 years, and 12-17 years. Using this categorization, changes in regional innovative capacity can be anticipated. For example, a decline in a region's innovative capacity can be expected when there is a decline in the share of the younger age group (0-5 years), particularly when the share of this group falls below the two older groups. On the other hand, when the share of the youngest group of patents is larger than the two older groups, it is expected that innovative capacity will rise in the future. Upon analyzing these patent age cycles, Suarez-Villa was able to provide another look at the multi-state regional inversion of the loci of invention patents, leading him to the conclusion that the effect of innovative capacity and of patent age cycles on long-term economic change and regional inversion occurs primarily through technological substitution, as newer inventions replace older ones in many activities, increasing efficiency and productivity and, eventually, income (Suarez-Villa, 1993, p.158).

Following the same trends as innovative capacity, Suarez-Villa also found that aggregate income rose the fastest within the Sunbelt region throughout the postwar period, with the result that Sunbelt's income surpassed that of the Northeast and Midwest just as it had done with innovative capacity. The Northeast's and Midwest's incomes rose during this period but not as rapidly as in the Sunbelt, and as with innovative capacity, the income trends of the two regions ran parallel to each other, with the Northeast maintaining a higher income level over the whole time period.

The work of Suarez-Villa shows that innovative capacity has profound effects on the economic growth and development of regional economies. The factors that influence the development of this innovative capacity, therefore, have considerable economic importance. In the chapter that follows, a model is developed that attempts to capture the role of these variables in the development of the innovation potential of one industry – the U.S. machine tool industry.

4 Innovation Potential: A Structured Inquiry

Introduction

The previous chapter showed the importance of innovation potential to economic growth and some of the factors that influence its development. I now focus on the role played by these factors in the development of the innovation potential of the U.S. machine tool industry at the metro-regional level. I begin by laying out the structure of the inquiry.

The Models

The model of metro-regional machine tool innovation potential to be estimated has the following general functional form:

$$(4.1) \qquad IP_r = f(UE_r, LE_r, DP_r, CE_r, GD_r, PHD_r, IR_r, IT_r, IDK_r)$$

where:

IP_r = machine tool industry innovation potential in region r
UE_r = urbanization economies in region r
LE_r = localization economies in region r
DP_r = federal government demand-pull in region r
CE_r = percent college educated in region r
GD_r = percent with a graduate degree in region r
PHD_r = percent with a Ph.D. in mechanical engineering produced in region r
IR_r = industrial restructuring (shift to services) in region r
IT_r = information technology investment in region r
IDK_r = invention derived knowledge (intra- and interindustry) in region r.

A description of the variables, including how they are operationalized, and their hypothesized effects, is given in table 4.1. Table 4.2 provides descriptive statistics for each of the variables. Ordinary least squares regression is used with each variable in natural logarithmic format in order to remedy the problems resulting from heteroskedasticity (see section 4.5).

In keeping with previous research (Acs and Audretsch, 1988, 1989; Feldman, 1992; Griliches, 1979; Jaffe, 1986, 1989; Mansfield, 1981), the model can be thought of as a production function in which innovation potential is being "produced" by the "inputs" of regional endowments. No assumptions are made about the values of the parameters.

The Patent Data

The main body of data consists of all U.S. machine tool patents granted from 1976 through 1992 (source: U.S. Patent and Trademark Office). As with all patent data, there exist two principal shortcomings associated with using these data. The first is that the patent data do not capture all inventions, as all inventions are not patented. The second is that all inventions are not of equal importance. Some inventions are simply slight adjustments in existing products or processes and thus, register small, if any, economic impact, while other inventions are quite revolutionary and register a relatively large economic impact.

There is no denying these criticisms. However, much research has been done testing the reliability of patent data as a measure of inventive activity, and many studies have concluded that patent data do provide a good measure of invention (Acs and Audretsch, 1989; Basberg, 1987; Comanor and Scherer, 1969; Griliches, 1990; Griliches, Pakes, and Hall, 1987; Narin, Noma, and Perry, 1987; Pakes and Griliches, 1984). As Suarez-Villa notes, "their availability, direct relationship with inventiveness, and largely objective evaluation standards, make them the single most important and reliable source of historical data on invention" (Suarez-Villa, 1993, p.148).

A remaining possible critique of the data set is that it only goes as far back as 1976. This means that many important inventions within this sector may not be included in the data. There is some merit to this critique. However, the data set is comprehensive, meaning that it contains all of the

Table 4.1-Metro-regional stimulants of innovation potential (unit of analysis = U.S. metropolitan areas)

Dependent Variable	Description
Metro-Regional Innovation Potential	Total U.S. machine tool patents created within metro-regions, 1990-1992 (#)

Independent Variables
{(+/-)=expected effect}

Agglomeration Economies

a. Urbanization Economies (+)	1990 metro-regional population
b. Localization Economies (+)	Metro-regional average annual machine tool output, 1982-1989 (1988$)

Federal Government Demand-Pull (+) — Average annual metro-regional receipt of federal spending on machine tools, 1985-1989

Human Capital

a. College Educated (+) — % of metro-regional population aged 25+ with 16 years of education

b. Graduate Degree (+) — % of metro-regional population aged 25+ with a graduate degree

c. Ph.D. in M.E. (+) — Ph.D. graduates in mechanical engineering produced locally, 1987-1992, as a % of 1987 local total employment

Industrial Restructuring

a. Shift to Services (+) — Rate of change in metro-regional producer services earnings share of total earnings, 1976-1990

Information Technology Investment (+) — Dollar value of installed multi-user computer networks cumulative within metro-regions as of 1-1-91

Invention-Derived Knowledge

a. Intraindustry (+) — Machine tool patents created within metro-regions lagged: 1976-1979, 1980-1982, 1983-1985, 1986-1989 (#)

b. Interindustry (+) — Semiconductor patents created within metro-regions lagged: 1976-1979, 1980-1982, 1983-1985, 1986-1989 (#)

Table 4.2-Descriptive statistics of variables

Machine Tool Variables	Mean	Standard Deviation	Min.	Max.
Innovation Potential (# of patents)	19.45	27.38	1	143
Urbanization Economies (1990 population)	2068313.73	2858371.48	339172	17953372
Localization Economies (Mach. tool output in thousands of 1988 $)	172362.59	324483.39	500	2137750
Federal Government Demand-Pull (Mach. tool procurement in thousands of $)	1478.42	2291.53	-92	8987
College Educated (%)	21.82	4.33	12.80	37
Graduate Degree (%)	7.71	2.06	3.80	15.80
Ph.D. Grads. in M.E. Produced Locally (%)	0.0054	0.0047	0.0005	0.0195
Shift to Services (%)	23.25	16.34	-22.35	65.25
Information Technology Investment (Multiuser computer networks in thousands of $)	1075280.93	1432618.50	99571	9028194
Invention-Derived Knowledge (# of patents)				
Machine Tools				
1976-1979	22.42	35.08	1	177
1980-1982	16.63	23.46	0	125
1983-1985	15.45	20.96	0	114
1986-1989	26.18	35.39	1	172
Semiconductors				
1976-1979	44.69	86.32	0	460
1980-1982	33.58	66.71	0	343
1983-1985	38.34	72.80	0	372
1986-1989	66.88	136	0	813

Table 4.2-(Continued)

Semiconductor Variables	Mean	Standard Deviation	Min.	Max.
Innovation Potential (# of patents)	58.22	123.79	1	808
Localization Economies (Semiconductor output in thousands of 1988 $)	511342.83	1070057.63	522	616975
Federal Government Demand-Pull (Semiconductor procurement in thousands of $)	2000.39	5272.90	-3436	29415
Ph.D. Grads. in E.E. Produced Locally (%)	0.0078	0.0074	0.0006	0.0366

NOTE: For a full description of the variables, see table 4.1.

U.S. machine tool patents for which the U.S. Patent and Trademark Office has complete data. Thus, all available data are being used.

The patent data set contains the following:
(1) Patent number
(2) Date the patent was issued
(3) Inventor(s)
(4) City and state of each inventor
(5) Assignee: company or person who owns the patent
(6) City and state of the assignee.
If a patent was issued to a foreign inventor or assignee, the country is given in place of the state. Thus, the data set contains domestic as well as foreign inventors and assignees (see table 1.1), but all patents were granted in the United States.

A machine tool patent was defined by the Patent and Trademark Office by identifying the patent classifications that are "entirely or substantially pertinent to the technology of interest" (U.S. Patent and Trademark Office, 1993, p.3). Those patents that fell into the machine tool classifications were included. Thus, the data contain patents for

machines for milling, planing, gear cutting, broaching, tearing or breaking, punching, turning, grinding, abrading, and making screws, nails or bolts. In

52

addition, tool changing apparatus is included. Also included are metal tools used in such machines, such as lathes, cutters and grinders. Other metal working apparatus in combination with shaping and/or assembling are also included. Patents which are found in classes which disclose cutting per se, e.g., not necessarily limited to metal, are not included (U.S. Patent and Trademark Office, 1993, p.2).

The date related to the patent is the date the patent was granted, rather than the date the application was filed for a patent.

A similar process was used to define semiconductor patents, used as the dependent variable in a model estimated for comparison with the machine tool analysis. The semiconductor patents as defined by the Patent and Trademark Office focus on the following technologies:

- active solid-state devices
- semiconductor device manufacturing processes
- solid-state electrical transmission or interconnection systems
- metal working processes and apparatus for making barrier layer or semiconductor devices
- etching processes and apparatus for making semiconductor devices
- semiconductor device systems for static information storage and retrieval
- metal treatment processes for making barrier layer stock material and semiconductor devices
- semiconductor laser devices
- single crystal growth crystallizers
- barrier layer device compositions
- vapor deposition coating apparatus
- liquid phase epitaxy coating apparatus
- single crystal formation methods
- imaging composition, process, or product, for making an electrical device
- photoelectric devices (U.S. Patent and Trademark Office, 1992, p.1).

As was done with the machine tool patent data, the date related to the patent is the date the patent was granted, rather than the date the application was filed for a patent.[1]

In order to describe the spatial distribution of innovation potential, the data are organized by metropolitan area, as defined in the 1990 census by the

---

[1] The original semiconductor data from the U.S. Patent and Trademark Office were organized by Daniel M. O'Brien.

U.S. Office of Management and Budget. Using the city and state of the inventors, the domestic patents are geo-coded into the metropolitan area [i.e., Consolidated Metropolitan Statistical Areas (CMSA), Metropolitan Statistical Areas (MSA), and New England County Metropolitan Areas (NECMA)] of the residence of the first inventor to yield a picture of the number of machine tool patents produced within each of the metropolitan areas of the United States for each year in the study.

The Dependent Variable

The dependent variable selected for analysis is the metro-regional innovation potential of the machine tool industry, defined operationally as the number of machine tool patents produced within the metropolitan area from 1990 through 1992.[2] If the variable had only been defined over a one-year period, significant year-to-year fluctuations would have caused a misrepresentation of the innovation potential within some regions. By covering a three-year period, the possible misrepresentation is dampened while the spatial variation in the variable is maintained.

The Independent Variables

As noted in section 4.1, above, nine independent variables were included in the general model formulation for exploration of their explanatory power.

Agglomeration Economies

In keeping with previous findings, agglomeration economies are hypothesized to exert a positive influence on regional innovation potential. The effects of two different kinds of agglomeration economies - urbanization economies and localization economies - are analyzed.

Urbanization economies Urbanization economies are economies realized by the firm as a result of the overall level of economic activity within the region.

---

[2] Suarez-Villa (1993) and Suarez-Villa and Hasnath (1993) used a similar conception in their works, except their closely related concept of innovative capacity was the total of all patents over a seventeen year period for multi-state regions.

Firms located within large regions derive these economies from the innovation-inducing infrastructures and

> The multiplicity of interaction among the large number of persons employed in secondary and tertiary industries in urban areas quickens the rate of technological invention and innovation...and increases the speed of dissemination of ideas and diffusion of skills (Goodall, 1972, p.36).

To capture the effects of urbanization economies on inventive capacity, the 1990 metropolitan area population level is entered as an explanatory variable (source: U.S. Department of Commerce – Bureau of Economic Analysis).

Localization economies   Localization economies available to a firm within a particular industry are achieved through the advantages created by the concentration of firms of that industry within a metropolitan area.   Firms involved in production will have considerable insight into where technological change is needed because they receive feedback from a variety of sources that guides their inventive efforts (Kline and Rosenberg, 1986). A concentration of firms of the same industry should magnify this feedback leading to more inventive activity. The competitive environment created by this concentration may also facilitate investment in the creation of new products and processes in an attempt to remain competitive.   Thus, it is expected that localization economies will positively influence innovation potential. These effects are operationalized as the localized average annual machine tool industry output from 1982-1989 (source: DRI/McGraw-Hill).

Federal Government Demand

The influence of demand-pull does not arise out of private sector demand alone. Given the size of the federal government within the United States and the volume of purchases that such a large government makes, it is expected that differences in federal government procurement of goods across regions should affect the differences in the innovation potential across these metro-regions. In particular, the federal government demands that the goods they purchase embody particular technologies which, through demand-pull, catalyzes inventive activity. For example, the demand from the government for interchangeable parts in their guns facilitated the invention of the milling machine (see chapter two). Changes in the federal government's demand could be expected, therefore, to have a direct influence on the innovation potential of an industry. This effect is measured as the average annual level of federal spending from 1985-1990 on machine tool goods (semiconductor goods) flowing to the metro-regions (source: *Federal Prime Contracts*, Eagle Eye Publishers).

Human Capital

The quality of the labor force within a metro-region should have a direct effect on the innovation potential of the region. Firms located within regions with a highly educated labor force are likely to be more innovative because they have easy access to a labor force equipped to both handle and produce technological advances. To capture the influence of human capital, three separate measures are operationalized, allowing for the measurement of three different higher-order "skill-levels" of the labor force: (1) the percent of the metro-regional population twenty-five years or older with at least sixteen years of education (source: Hall and Slater, 1996), (2) the percent of the metro-regional population twenty-five years or older holding a graduate degree (source: Labich, 1993), and (3) the number of Ph.D. graduates in mechanical engineering for the academic year 1987-1988 to 1991-1992 produced locally as a percent of 1987 employment (source: Goldberger, Maher, and Flattau, 1995).

Part of the infrastructure that influences inventive activity is the educational institutions within the region. Colleges and universities are the producers of a highly skilled workforce with the abilities to effectively work in an environment of rapid technological change. These are also the institutions that produce the research scientists who play a large role in creating the inventions in both the academic and private sectors. These human capital variables will also capture this influence.

This is not a perfectly clean relationship, though, since many students are educated in one region and move to another one to work. The Ph.D. variable gets closest to capturing this influence since it directly measures the *local* production of doctorates in mechanical engineering by universities within the region. Local universities with a Ph.D. program in mechanical engineering are going to be conducting research, which may produce patents that add to the machine tool indsutry's innovation potential. These graduate programs will also be supplying the region with doctorates in mechanical engineering who are likely to be engaged in the research that creates machine tool inventions. Furthermore, such universities will also have undergraduate programs that, along with their graduate programs, supply the region with skilled labor. Therefore, the Ph.D. production variable is a good indicator of the influence a local university can have on the development of machine tool innovation potential at the metro-regional level.

Industrial Restructuring

For many decades, the United States economy has been restructuring itself from a goods-producing economy to a services economy. For example, according to *The Economist* (19 March 1994, p.91), 27% of America's workers were employed in manufacturing in 1970, but by 1993, only 16% were employed in this sector. On the other hand, over this same time period, the percentage of employment in the services sector had increased from 66% to 78%. There has even been fundamental restructuring within the manufacturing sector such that 75% of value-added created within this sector is due to services (Quinn, 1986). The upshot is that the boundary between goods production and services production has become blurred. What effect does this restructuring have on the innovation potential of the machine tool industry? At first glance, it appears that this would have a negative impact given the shrinking importance of the manufacturing sector. On the other hand, the growth of the services sector has created the need for the development and manufacture of new products (e.g. the creation of the fax machine and ATM machines) that require new machine tools to cut and form metal in new ways.

Thus, the growth of the services sector may influence the development of innovation potential through the demand-pull effect. To capture the influence of the growth of this sector, the rate of change in the producer services[3] share of total metro-regional earnings over the time period of 1976 through 1990 was calculated (source: U.S. Department of Commerce - Bureau of Economic Analysis).

---

[3] The definition of producer services was taken from Noyelle and Stanback (1983). Producer services is defined to include finance, insurance, and real estate (SIC 60 to 67), business services (SIC 73), legal services (SIC 81), membership organizations (SIC 86), miscellaneous services (SIC 89), and social services (SIC 83).

Information Technology Investment

It is hypothesized that those regions with a greater investment in information technology will provide better support for the inventive process. Recent research (*The Economist*, 22 January 1994; Hicks and Nivin, 1994) has shown that investment in information technology yields returns in the form of increased workers' productivity.

But, will investment of this kind increase the productivity of machine tool patent production? It is hypothesized that it will. This is because investment in information technology will enhance the flow of information and ideas, which is vitally important in the inventive process. Investment in this technology is measured as the dollar value of installed multi-user computer network systems cumulative as of January 1, 1991 (source: International Data Corporation).

Invention-Derived Knowledge

Inventions patented in the past may influence the rate of invention because they provide new knowledge that may allow for further technological advance. Furthermore, previous invention patents may also influence the direction of inventive activity by shaping the inventors' preferences for future developments. In other words, past inventions add to the stock of useful knowledge which enables new inventions and which shapes the direction of inventive activity. It is through these mechanisms that past inventive success energizes future inventive success. Thus, there should exist a positive relationship between previously patented inventions and metro-regional innovation potential.

Beggs found that there exist five and eight year lags from patented invention to patented invention, and that "inventions in one industry may lead to follow-up inventions in other industries, but the transmission process will be slower" (Beggs, 1984, pp.164-165) than if the inventions were in the same industry. In order to discover the lag structure of the transmission process within the machine tool industry, the sum total of the number of machine tool invention patents over four time periods - 1976-1979, 1980-1982, 1983-1985, and 1986-1989 - is entered into the model. These time periods correspond to the different stages of the business cycle and thus, control for whatever impact the business cycle would have on inventive activities. For instance, 1976-

1979 was a period of stagflation; 1980-1982 was a recessionary period; 1983-1985 was a period of rapid growth; and 1986-1989 was a period of slowing growth leading into a recession. To discover the lag structure of the transmission process *across* industries, the sum totals of semiconductor invention patents over the same four time periods also are entered as explanatory variables. This should yield a picture of the extent to which this process occurs both across and within industries and the time period necessary for the process to yield results.

Measurement Issues

All of the variables in the model are entered in their natural logarithmic forms. This is due to the presence of heteroscedasticity, which is clearly evident in the graphs shown in appendix A. The presence of heteroscedasticity is not surprising because "as a matter of fact, in cross-sectional data involving heterogeneous units, heteroscedasticity may be the rule rather than the exception" (Gujarati, 1988, p.327).

One way to solve the problem is to transform the variables into natural logarithms (Gujarati, 1988). Thus, the problem of inefficient estimates caused by the heteroscedasticity was addressed by taking the natural log of all of the variables - both dependent and independent. Graphs in which only one of the variables was in a logarithmic form were analyzed, but that did not appear to be as good a solution as taking the logarithm of both variables. This log-linear transformation also has the added advantage of rendering the coefficients as elasticities (Greene, 1993; Gujarati, 1988).

As shown in the accompanying graphs in appendix A, taking the natural logarithm of both the dependent and independent variable yields a more "standard" scatterplot by removing the heteroscedasticity and by spreading the cluster of observations near the origin. This was true in all cases.

A Breusch-Pagan test for heteroscedasticity was also run for the model given in table 5.1. It was assumed that the error variance, σ_r^2, is a linear function of all of the nonstochastic variables:

(4.2) $\sigma_r^2 = a_1 + a_2(UE_r) + a_2(LE_r) + a_3(DP_r) + a_4(CE_r) + a_5(GD_r) + a_6(PHD_r) + a_7(IR_r) + a_8(IT_r).$

The Breusch-Pagan test statistic was calculated to be 2.65667, which is not significant at the 5% level of significance, indicating that the log-linear transformation remedied the heteroscedasticity.

The Development of Innovation Potential Across Industries

Do the factors influencing the development of the innovation potential of the machine tool industry have the same effect on the development of the innovation potential of other industries? To provide at least a partial answer to this question, models that mirror those for the machine tool innovation potential are also estimated for the innovation potential of the semiconductor industry.

Operationally, the urbanization economies, college educated, graduate degree, industrial restructuring, and IT investment variables in the semiconductor models are all measured the exact same way as they are in the machine tool models. The only changes made to the other variables were to make them more appropriate to the semiconductor industry. For instance, the innovation potential of the semiconductor industry is measured as the total number of semiconductor patents granted to inventors residing within the metro-region from 1990 through 1992. Localization economies were operationalized as the average annual semiconductor output over the period of 1982 through 1989. To measure federal government demand-pull, average annual spending on semiconductors from 1985 through 1989 was used. In the semiconductor models, Ph.D. graduates in electrical engineering produced locally as a percentage of 1987 employment was included. Lastly, the influence of intraindustry invention-derived knowledge on the innovation potential of the semiconductor industry used semiconductor patents over the same four lagged time periods.

5 Factors Influencing the Development of Innovation Potential

The Geographic Distribution of Machine Tool Innovation Potential

As shown in table 1.1, 9,736 patents were granted to resident inventors of the U.S from 1976-1992. Of these, 8,529 (87.6%) were granted to inventors residing in U.S. metropolitan areas. The innovation potential of the U.S. metro-regions used in this study ranged from a low of 1 to a high of 143 patents (see table 4.2). The five regions with the highest machine tool innovation potential are (in order from highest to lowest): Detroit-Ann Arbor, Michigan; Los Angeles-Anaheim-Riverside, California; New York-Northern New Jersey-Long Island, New York-New Jersey; Chicago-Gary-Lake County, IL-IN-WI; and Minneapolis-St. Paul, Minnesota-Wisconsin. In figure 5.1, the 3-year moving averages of the fluctuations in machine tool patent activity within these five regions are presented. Table B.1 in appendix B shows the machine tool patent activity of the top twenty-five regions ranked by innovation potential. From this table, it is clear that Minneapolis-St. Paul was not a top five producer of machine tool patents in 1976, but by 1992, it had become a top five producer of machine tool patents. This rise in "output" is indicated in figure 5.1 also. The other four regions were, for the most part, one of the top five producers of machine tool patents every year from 1976 through 1992. Comparing 1976 rankings of "production" with those in 1992, we can see that Detroit overtook Los Angeles as leading producer of machine tool patents in 1992. The same occurred between Chicago and New York with Chicago taking over the third spot in 1992. Of the top five regions, the most dramatic increases came in Detroit and Minneapolis, while the other three regions experienced declines across the 1976-1992 period.

61

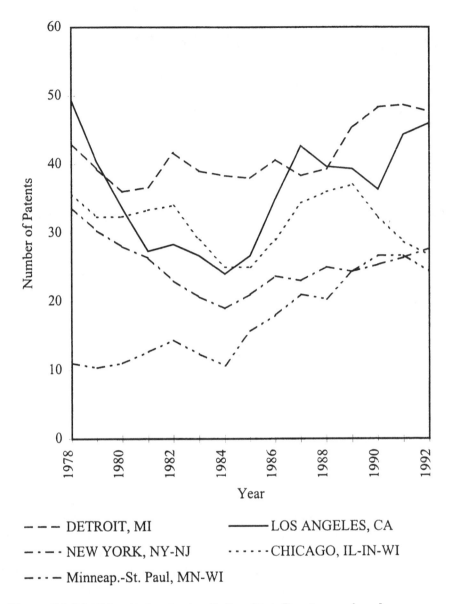

Year

- - - DETROIT, MI   ——— LOS ANGELES, CA

- · - · NEW YORK, NY-NJ   · · · · · · CHICAGO, IL-IN-WI

- · · - Minneap.-St. Paul, MN-WI

Figure 5.1 Machine tool patent activity of top 5 metro-regions by innovation potential (3 year moving average)

These five regions accounted for 26.8% of the machine tool patenting activity of domestic inventors, and the top twenty-five regions accounted for 55.9% of this activity from 1976 through 1992. While a sizable portion of machine tool patenting occurs within these leading regions, there still remains considerable variation in this activity across regions.

Two questions still remain, though. First, what accounts for the variation in innovation potential across regions, and second, are these influences similar across industries? It is to these two questions that we now turn.

Trial and Error Model Development

The final model format shown in table 5.12 (after page 130) was reached through a process of trial and error in which statistical problems were discovered and addressed. This section documents that process.

Initial results of estimating the model described in the preceding chapter are shown in table 5.1. None of the variables are significant, but the adjusted R^2 is high, indicating problems due to multicollinearity. There is significant correlation among the invention-derived knowledge variables. This is problematic when both the invention-derived knowledge (IDK) variable (e.g., patents 1986-1989) and the dependent variable (patents 1990-1992) are driven by the same stimuli, because the coefficient on the IDK variable captures the effects of the stimuli, too. One solution is simply to remove the IDK variables from the model.

Is this solution justified in this case? Will other methods allow us to keep these variables in the models? We now turn to answering these questions.

First, what if, instead of removing all of the IDK variables, we removed all but one from the model? This approach was tried in the model in table 5.1 with the results reported in appendix C and on models one through three in table 5.12. The results are the same for either specification. Since the models in table 5.12 are the final result of handling other problems (to be discussed shortly) and thus, provide the optimum opportunity for inclusion of these variables, only these results are reported (see tables 5.2-5.5). The results of applying this approach to the model in table 5.1 can be found in appendix C.

63

Table 5.1-Model of machine tool innovation potential

Dependent Variable: Machine Tool Innovation Potential (ln)

Variable	Coefficient
Intercept	-0.409
	(-0.114)
Agglomeration Economies	
Urbanization Economies (ln)	-0.223
	(-0.628)
Localization Economies (ln)	-0.029
	(-0.226)
Federal Government Demand-Pull (ln)	0.087
	(0.792)
Human Capital	
College Educated (ln)	1.413
	(1.281)
Graduate Degree (ln)	-0.825
	(-1.040)
Ph.D. Graduates in Mechanical Engineering	-0.041
Produced Locally (ln)	(-0.257)
Industrial Restructuring	
Shift to Services (ln)	-0.004
	(-0.023)
Information Technology Investment (ln)	0.035
	(0.099)
Invention-Derived Knowledge	
Intraindustry	
1976-1979 (ln)	-0.319
	(-1.060)
1980-1982 (ln)	0.203
	(0.662)
1983-1985 (ln)	0.078
	(0.222)
1986-1989 (ln)	0.929
	(2.021)
Interindustry	
1976-1979 (ln)	-0.294
	(1.098)
1980-1982 (ln)	0.102
	(0.373)
1983-1985 (ln)	0.617
	(1.569)
1986-1989 (ln)	-0.308
	(-1.322)
Adjusted R^2	0.744
df	31

*=significance at the 5% level
**=significance at the 1% level
Numbers in parentheses are t-scores

When the results shown in tables 5.2-5.5 are compared with those in table 5.12, it appears that inclusion of any IDK variable suppresses the effects of the other variables. For instance, in models one through three of table 5.12, urbanization economies are significant in all, but in models one through three of tables 5.2-5.5, the variable is not significant in eight out of twelve models. The localization economies variable is significant in both models one and two of table 5.12, but it is not significant in any of the twelve models shown in models one through three of tables 5.2-5.5. Furthermore, both the graduate degree and Ph.D. variables in models two and three, respectively, of table 5.12 are significant, but with the IDK variables included, the graduate degree variable is insignificant in three out of four of the models, and the Ph.D. variable is insignificant in all of the models.

Another possible method of handling the multicollinearity among these variables is to impose a lag structure by depreciating the effect of the IDK variables over each of the time periods and summing the results of the depreciated values into one IDK variable covering the entire 1976-1989 time period. In doing this, it is assumed that the effects of intraindustry invention-derived knowledge depreciated over time in a linear manner. The depreciated intraindustry IDK variable was calculated as follows:

(5.1) $IDK_{M,1976-89} = (IDK_{M,1976-79})(.2) + (IDK_{M,1980-82})(.4) + (IDK_{M,1983-85})(.6) + (IDK_{M,1986-89})(.8)$

where M denotes machine tool IDK. In calculating the depreciated interindustry IDK variable, it was assumed that semicnoductor patents granted in the 1986-1989 time period would have the least effect, and the 1983-1985 stock of semiconductor patents would have the largest effect. This was based on the hypothesis that knowledge embodied in inventions is transferred at a slower rate across industries (Beggs 1984). The depreciated interindustry IDK variable was calculated as follows:

(5.2) $IDK_{S,1976-89} = (IDK_{S,1976-79})(.4) + (IDK_{S,1980-82})(.6) + (IDK_{S,1983-85})(.8) + (IDK_{S,1986-89})(.2)$

where S denotes semiconductor IDK.

Table 5.2-Results of including 1986-1989 IDK

Dependent Variable: Machine Tool Innovation Potential (ln)

Variable	Model 1	Model 2	Model 3
Intercept	-1.322	0.853	-2.092
	(-0.642)	(0.455)	(-0.721)
Agglomeration Economies			
Urbanization Economies (ln)	0.049	-0.058	0.134
	(0.380)	(-0.440)	(0.754)
Localization Economies (ln)	0.064	0.054	0.017
	(1.074)	(0.820)	(0.266)
Federal Government Demand-	-0.012	0.017	-0.017
Pull (ln)	(-0.216)	(0.287)	(-0.252)
Human Capital			
College Educated (ln)	0.280	-	-
	(0.647)		
Graduate Degree (ln)	-	-0.009	-
		(-0.028)	
Ph.D. Grads. in Mech. Eng.	-	-	0.092
Produced Locally (ln)			(0.846)
Industrial Restructuring			
Shift to Services (ln)	-0.175	-0.171	-0.145
	(-1.741)	(-1.627)	(-1.213)
Invention-Derived Knowledge			
Intraindustry			
1986-1989 (ln)	0.791	0.862	0.826
	(7.209**)	(7.060**)	(5.427**)
Adjusted R^2	0.794	0.790	0.783
df	54	44	38

*=significance at the 5% level
**=significance at the 1% level
Numbers in parentheses are t-scores

66

Table 5.2-(Continued)

Dependent Variable: Machine Tool Innovation Potential (ln)

Variable	Model 4	Model 5	Model 6
Intercept	-5.442	-3.624	-8.774
	(-1.754)	(-1.309)	(-2.297*)
Agglomeration Economies			
Urbanization Economies (ln)	0.354	0.198	0.529
	(2.078*)	(1.048)	(2.151*)
Localization Economies (ln)	0.124	0.158	0.086
	(1.476)	(1.685)	(0.975)
Federal Government Demand-	0.042	0.050	0.069
Pull (ln)	(0.564)	(0.577)	(0.705)
Human Capital			
College Educated (ln)	0.179	-	-
	(0.274)		
Graduate Degree (ln)	-	0.349	-
		(0.694)	
Ph.D. Grads. in Mech. Eng.	-	-	0.235
Produced Locally (ln)			(1.648)
Industrial Restructuring			
Shift to Services (ln)	0.058	0.168	-0.007
	(0.438)	(0.114)	(-0.045)
Invention-Derived Knowledge			
Interindustry			
1986-1989 (ln)	0.234	0.244	0.200
	(2.503*)	(2.412*)	(1.685)
Adjusted R^2	0.621	0.580	0.618
Df	54	44	38

*=significance at the 5% level
**=significance at the 1% level
Numbers in parentheses are t-scores

Table 5.3-Results of including 1983-1985 IDK

Dependent Variable: Machine Tool Innovation Potential

Variable	Model 1	Model 2	Model 3
Intercept	-5.557	-3.275	-1.525
	(-2.493*)	(-1.659)	(-0.430)
Agglomeration Economies			
Urbanization Economies (ln)	0.306	0.169	0.228
	(2.186*)	(1.151)	(1.161)
Localization Economies (ln)	0.075	0.081	-0.008
	(1.011)	(0.989)	(-0.100)
Federal Government Demand-Pull (ln)	-0.048	-0.059	-0.047
	(-0.727)	(-0.833)	(-0.619)
Human Capital			
College Educated (ln)	0.630	-	-
	(1.226)		
Graduate Degree (ln)	-	0.763	-
		(2.054*)	
Ph.D. Grads. in Mech. Eng. Produced Locally (ln)	-	-	-0.020
			(-0.146)
Industrial Restructuring			
Shift to Services (ln)	0.017	0.016	-0.090
	(0.145)	(0.128)	(-0.684)
Invention-Derived Knowledge Intraindustry			
1983-1985	0.543	0.607	0.746
	(4.553**)	(4.603**)	(4.303**)
Adjusted R^2	0.701	0.689	0.736
df	54	44	38

*=significance at the 5% level
**=significance at the 1% level
Numbers in parentheses are t-scores

Table 5.3-(Continued)

Dependent Variable: Machine Tool Innovation Potential

Variable	Model 4	Model 5	Model 6
Intercept	-5.719	-3.871	-7.495
	(-1.890)	(-1.337)	(-2.056*)
Agglomeration Economies			
Urbanization Economies (ln)	0.340	0.235	0.443
	(1.960)	(1.243)	(1.897)
Localization Economies (ln)	0.121	0.146	0.059
	(1.434)	(1.458)	(0.675)
Federal Government Demand-	0.045	0.050	0.094
Pull (ln)	(0.595)	(0.557)	(0.984)
Human Capital			
College Educated (ln)	0.365	-	-
	(0.589)		
Graduate Degree (ln)	-	0.352	-
		(0.669)	
Ph.D. Grads. in Mech. Eng.	-	-	0.238
Produced Locally (ln)			(1.780)
Industrial Restructuring			
Shift to Services (ln)	0.067	0.005	-0.004
	(0.508)	(0.035)	(-0.024)
Invention-Derived Knowledge			
Interindustry			
1983-1985	0.230	0.237	0.261
	(2.496*)	(2.140*)	(2.293*)
Adjusted R^2	0.620	0.568	0.643
df	54	44	38

*=significance at the 5% level
**=significance at the 1% level
Numbers in parentheses are t-scores

69

Table 5.4-Results of including 1980-1982 IDK

Dependent Variable: Machine Tool Innovation Potential

Variable	Model 1	Model 2	Model 3
Intercept	-5.623	-1.826	-5.503
	(-2.184*)	(-0.728)	(-1.339)
Agglomeration Economies			
Urbanization Economies (ln)	0.359	0.154	0.455
	(2.377*)	(0.938)	(2.059*)
Localization Economies (ln)	0.051	0.013	0.002
	(0.587)	(0.126)	(0.024)
Federal Government Demand-Pull (ln)	0.007	0.019	-0.020
	(0.098)	(0.248)	(-0.229)
Human Capital			
College Educated (ln)	0.520	-	-
	(0.927)		
Graduate Degree (ln)	-	0.364	-
		(0.847)	
Ph.D. Grads. in Mech. Eng. Produced Locally (ln)	-	-	0.108
			(0.698)
Industrial Restructuring			
Shift to Services (ln)	-0.078	-0.088	-0.116
	(-0.598)	(-0.647)	(-0.766)
Invention-Derived Knowledge			
Intraindustry			
1980-1982	0.477	0.656	0.512
	(3.409**)	(3.689**)	(2.448*)
Adjusted R^2	0.655	0.643	0.650
df	54	44	38

*=significance at the 5% level
**=significance at the 1% level
Numbers in parentheses are t-scores

Table 5.4-(Continued)

Dependent Variable: Machine Tool Innovation Potential

Variable	Model 4	Model 5	Model 6
Intercept	-5.562	-1.932	-9.150
	(-1.873)	(-0.651)	(-2.446*)
Agglomeration Economies			
Urbanization Economies (ln)	0.324	0.126	0.554
	(1.874)	(0.658)	(2.307*)
Localization Economies (ln)	0.125	0.139	0.103
	(1.511)	(1.516)	(1.212)
Federal Government Demand-Pull (ln)	0.049	0.059	0.061
	(0.654)	(0.703)	(0.633)
Human Capital			
College Educated (ln)	0.397	-	-
	(0.654)		
Graduate Degree (ln)	-	0.152	-
		(0.297)	
Ph.D. Grads. in Mech. Eng. Produced Locally (ln)	-	-	0.250
			(1.785)
Industrial Restructuring			
Shift to Services (ln)	0.041	-0.021	-0.047
	(0.317)	(-0.145)	(-0.294)
Invention-Derived Knowledge			
Interindustry			
1980-1982	0.236	0.306	0.187
	(2.645*)	(2.828**)	(1.620)
Adjusted R^2	0.626	0.600	0.615
df	54	44	38

*=significance at the 5% level
**=significance at the 1% level
Numbers in parentheses are t-scores

Table 5.5-Results of including 1976-1979 IDK

Dependent Variable: Machine Tool Innovation Potential

Variable	Model 1	Model 2	Model 3
Intercept	-5.208	-2.468	-6.160
	(-2.387*)	(-1.033)	(-1.769)
Agglomeration Economies			
Urbanization Economies (ln)	0.228	0.178	0.441
	(1.597)	(1.102)	(2.187*)
Localization Economies (ln)	0.039	0.034	0.021
	(0.522)	(0.343)	(0.247)
Federal Government Demand-Pull (ln)	-0.010	-0.015	-0.026
	(-0.156)	(-0.202)	(-0.310)
Human Capital			
College Educated (ln)	0.902	-	-
	(1.813)		
Graduate Degree (ln)	-	0.474	-
		(1.131)	
Ph.D. Grads. in Mech. Eng. Produced Locally (ln)	-	-	0.181
			(1.374)
Industrial Restructuring			
Shift to Services (ln)	-0.063	-0.078	-0.128
	(-0.545)	(-0.578)	(-0.872)
Invention-Derived Knowledge			
Intraindustry			
1976-1979	0.600	0.607	0.512
	(4.909**)	(3.674**)	(2.955**)
Adjusted R^2	0.715	0.642	0.673
df	54	44	38

*=significance at the 5% level
**=significance at the 1% level
Numbers in parentheses are t-scores

72

Table 5.5-(Continued)

Dependent Variable: Machine Tool Innovation Potential

Variable	Model 4	Model 5	Model 6
Intercept	-7.882	-4.947	-10.971
	(-2.474*)	(-1.585)	(-3.292**)
Agglomeration Economies			
Urbanization Economies (ln)	0.453	0.288	0.660
	(2.549*)	(1.449)	(3.008**)
Localization Economies (ln)	0.157	0.198	0.103
	(1.788)	(2.029*)	(1.157)
Federal Government Demand-Pull (ln)	0.030	0.030	0.053
	(0.378)	(0.325)	(0.530)
Human Capital			
College Educated (ln)	0.576	-	-
	(0.881)		
Graduate Degree (ln)	-	0.469	-
		(0.826)	
Ph.D. Grads. in Mech. Eng. Produced Locally (ln)	-	-	0.310
			(2.281*)
Industrial Restructuring			
Shift to Services (ln)	0.006	-0.074	-0.063
	(0.047)	(-0.479)	(-0.388)
Invention-Derived Knowledge			
Interindustry 1976-1979	0.134	0.174	0.138
	(1.418)	(1.481)	(1.253)
Adjusted R^2	0.588	0.542	0.603
df	54	44	38

*=significance at the 5% level
**=significance at the 1% level
Numbers in parentheses are t-scores

The natural logarithm of these variables was used in the models. The results indicate that the IDK variable is highly significant, but it is still acting as a suppressor of the other independent variables (see table 5.6).

Thus, it is still the case that the strong relationship between future innovation potential and past innovation potential suppresses the influences of the other variables.[1] This indicates that 1990-1992 innovation potential is a function of 1986-1989 innovation potential, but in both time periods, innovation potential is driven by the same variables.[2] Hence,

(5.3) $IP_{1990-92} = f(IP_{1986-89}, UE, LE, DP, HC, IR, IT)$

and

(5.4) $IP_{1986-89} = f(UE, LE, DP, HC, IR, IT)$

where:

$IP_{1990-92}$ = 1990-1992 innovation potential
$IP_{1986-89}$ = 1986-1989 innovation potential
UE = urbanization economies
LE = localization economies
DP = federal government demand-pull
HC = human capital
IR = industrial restructuring
IT = information technology investment.

In equation 5.3, the effects of UE, LE, DP, HC, IR, and IT explain the variation in $IP_{1986-89}$, as shown in equation 5.4, causing a suppressor effect.

Furthermore, there is circularity in this relationship because while agglomeration economies and human capital drive innovation potential, for example, innovation potential also influences agglomeration economies and

---

[1] Since the IDK variables are lagged dependent variables, they are, in effect, also measures of past innovation potential.
[2] Models one through three in table 5.12 were estimated using each of the IDK variables as the dependent variable. The results verified that each of the IDK variables are also driven by the other explanatory variables.

74

Table 5.6-Results of including depreciated IDK

Dependent Variable: Machine Tool Innovation Potential

Variable	Model 1	Model 2	Model 3
Intercept	-1.712	0.547	-0.344
	(-0.834)	(0.293)	(-0.158)
Agglomeration Economies			
Urbanization Economies (ln)	0.057	-0.055	0.049
	(0.442)	(-0.413)	(0.256)
Localization Economies (ln)	0.004	-0.024	-0.041
	(0.057)	(-0.326)	(-0.580)
Federal Government Demand-Pull (ln)	-0.016	0.004	-0.031
	(-0.287)	(0.062)	(-0.446)
Human Capital			
College Educated (ln)	0.315	-	-
	(0.723)		
Graduate Degree (ln)	-	0.097	-
		(0.294)	
Ph.D. Grads. in Mech. Eng. Produced Locally (ln)	-	-	-0.008
			(-0.070)
Industrial Restructuring			
Shift to Services (ln)	-0.136	-0.124	-0.130
	(-1.359)	(-1.185)	(-1.084)
Depreciated IDK			
Intraindustry			
1976-1989	0.891	0.983	0.969
	(7.062**)	(6.932**)	(5.369*)
Adjusted R^2	0.790	0.786	0.781
df	54	44	38

*=significance at the 5% level
**=significance at the 1% level
Numbers in parentheses are t-scores

Table 5.6-(Continued)

Dependent Variable: Machine Tool Innovation Potential

Variable	Model 4	Model 5	Model 6
Intercept	-3.319	-0.288	-0.927
	(-1.531)	(-0.142)	(-0.387)
Agglomeration Economies			
Urbanization Economies (ln)	0.155	0.011	0.128
	(1.135)	(0.076)	(0.617)
Localization Economies (ln)	0.002	-0.043	-0.053
	(0.025)	(-0.513)	(-0.666)
Federal Government Demand-Pull (ln)	-0.020	-0.012	-0.043
	(-0.344)	(-0.192)	(-0.574)
Human Capital			
College Educated (ln)	0.499	-	-
	(1.055)		
Graduate Degree (ln)	-	0.283	-
		(0.797)	
Ph.D. Grads. in Mech. Eng. Produced Locally (ln)	-	-	-0.015
			(-0.114)
Industrial Restructuring			
Shift to Services (ln)	-0.090	-0.081	-0.129
	(-0.827)	(-0.715)	(-1.000)
Depreciated IDK			
Interindustry			
1976-1989	0.787	0.933	0.902
	(5.832**)	(5.834**)	(4.490**)
Adjusted R^2	0.749	0.744	0.745
df	54	44	38

*=significance at the 5% level
**=significance at the 1% level
Numbers in parentheses are t-scores

human capital. This feedback mechanism imparts a certain level of "momentum" to inventive activity. Those regions that were proficient at producing machine tool patents and have built-up a storehouse of knowledge embodied in the patents of the past will have a momentum that gives the region the ability to persist in their inventive proficiency in the future.

Regardless of the methods used, the IDK variables act as suppressors, and thus, they are limiting what can be learned from these models. The only solution is to remove them completely, so the other variables can emerge and be recognized.

Having removed the IDK variables, the model shown in table 5.7 was estimated. The results are again unremarkable. All explanatory variables are insignificant, but the adjusted R^2 is still fairly high, indicating that multicollinearity is still a problem. If we look at the simple correlations of these independent variables in table 5.8, we see that the Pearson's correlation coefficient between the information technology investment variable and the urbanization economies variable is 0.8735. Believing this to be quite high and the source of some problem within the model, the IT investment variable was dropped from the model, with the results shown in table 5.9. As suspected, this variable was causing problems, as indicated by the fact that the coefficient for urbanization economies changed signs and became significant.

The models also were run with the human capital variables separated. Two sets of these models were estimated. One with both the urbanization economies and IT investment variables included (table 5.10) and the other with urbanization economies omitted (table 5.11). When these results are compared with those in the final models, it is apparent that a problem with the correlations between the IT investment variables and other variables remained, even in these models. This is due to the fact that other variables become significant with the removal of the IT variable.

Using the mean square error criterion, the validity of dropping the IT investment variable was tested. Operationally, this is equivalent to calculating a nested F statistic (Kmenta, 1986, p.594), where the model in table 5.9 is nested in the model in table 5.7. According to Kmenta (1986), if $F \leq 1$, the model in table 5.9, where the IT variable has been dropped, is chosen at a significance level greater than 5%. The calculated F statistic is 0.2703, indicating that it is appropriate to drop the IT investment variable.

It also seems reasonable to suspect that the human capital variables are highly correlated with one another. This is, in fact, the case between the

Table 5.7-Results of excluding IDK

Dependent Variable: Machine Tool Innovation Potential (ln)

Variable	Coefficient
Intercept	-6.302
	(-1.879)
Agglomeration Economies	
Urbanization Economies (ln)	-0.083
	(-0.206)
Localization Economies (ln)	0.178
	(1.700)
Federal Government Demand-Pull (ln)	-0.012
	(-0.112)
Human Capital	
College Educated (ln)	0.512
	(0.424)
Graduate Degree (ln)	-0.324
	(-0.412)
Ph.D. Graduates in Mechanical Engineering	0.250
Produced Locally	(1.540)
Industrial Restructuring	
Shift to Services (ln)	0.039
	(0.214)
Information Technology Investment (ln)	0.652
	(1.710)
Adjusted R^2	0.553
df	31

*=significance at the 5% level
**=significance at the 1% level
Numbers in parentheses are t-scores

Table 5.8-Pearson correlation coefficients (all variables in natural log form)

	Innovation Potential	Urbanization Economies	Localization Economies	Federal Govt. Demand-Pull
Innovation Potential	1.0000	0.7324**	0.6234**	0.5402**
Urbanization Economies	0.7324**	1.0000	0.5492**	0.5759**
Localization Economies	0.6234**	0.5492**	1.0000	0.6666**
Federal Govt. Demand-Pull	0.5402**	0.5759**	0.6666**	1.0000
College Educated	0.3259**	0.3521**	0.0242	0.1001
Graduate Degree	0.3513**	0.3407*	0.0059	0.1332
Ph.D. in Mech. Eng.	0.0143	-0.2612	-0.1056	-0.1534
Industrial Restructuring	0.2112	0.1848	0.1741	0.2835*
IT Investment	0.7328**	0.8735**	0.5209**	0.5318**
Intraindustry IDK				
1976-1979	0.8392**	0.7441**	0.7317**	0.6151**
1980-1982	0.7782**	0.6909**	0.7030**	0.6062**
1983-1985	0.8248**	0.7053**	0.6897**	0.6425**
1986-1989	0.8667**	0.7675**	0.6755**	0.5995**
Interindustry IDK				
1976-1979	0.7325**	0.7485**	0.5206**	0.4034**
1980-1982	0.7391**	0.7332**	0.4935**	0.3912**
1983-1985	0.7418**	0.7147**	0.4965**	0.3970**
1986-1989	0.7332**	0.7335**	0.4630**	0.3904**

Table 5.8-(Continued)

	College Educated	Graduate Degree	Ph.D. in Mech. Eng.	Industrial Restructuring	IT Investment
Innovation Potential	0.3259**	0.3513**	0.0143	0.2112	0.7328**
Urbanization Economies	0.3521**	0.3407*	-0.2612	0.1848	0.8735**
Localization Economies	0.0242	0.0059	-0.1056	0.1741	0.5209**
Federal Govt. Demand-Pull	0.1001	0.1332	-0.1534	0.2835*	0.5318**
College Educated	1.0000	0.8384**	0.1455	-0.1045	0.4695**
Graduate Degree	0.8384**	1.0000	0.3288*	-0.0043	0.4493**
Ph.D. in Mech. Eng.	0.1455	0.3288*	1.0000	0.0477	-0.1662
Industrial Restructuring	-0.1045	-0.0043	0.0477	1.0000	0.1858
IT Investment	0.4695**	0.4493**	-0.1662	0.1858	1.0000
Intraindustry IDK					
1976-1979	0.2316	0.2912*	-0.0409	0.3069**	0.7033**
1980-1982	0.2558*	0.2702*	0.0041	0.3146**	0.6827**
1983-1985	0.2682*	0.2563	0.1112	0.3054**	0.7239**
1986-1989	0.2886*	0.3850**	-0.0623	0.2632*	0.7420**
Interindustry IDK					
1976-1979	0.4355**	0.5402**	-0.0786	0.2106	0.7451**
1980-1982	0.4267**	0.5491**	0.0663	0.1601	0.7023**
1983-1985	0.4741**	0.5154**	-0.0083	0.1152	0.7219**
1986-1989	0.5344**	0.5255**	0.0875	0.0903	0.7154**

Table 5.8-(Continued)

	Intraindustry IDK 1976-1979	Intraindustry IDK 1980-1982	Intraindustry IDK 1983-1985	Intraindustry IDK 1986-1989
Innovation Potential	0.8392**	0.7782**	0.8248**	0.8667**
Urbanization Economies	0.7441**	0.6909**	0.7053**	0.7675**
Localization Economies	0.7317**	0.7030**	0.6897**	0.6755**
Federal Govt. Demand-Pull	0.6151**	0.6062**	0.6425**	0.5995**
College Educated	0.2316	0.2558*	0.2682*	0.2886*
Graduate Degree	0.2912*	0.2707*	0.2563	0.3850**
Ph.D. in Mech. Eng.	-0.0409	0.0041	0.1112	-0.0623
Industrial Restructuring	0.3069**	0.3146**	0.3054**	0.2632*
IT Investment	0.7033**	0.6827**	0.7239**	0.7420**
Intraindustry Idk				
1976-1979	1.0000	0.8917**	0.8713**	0.8512**
1980-1982	0.8917**	1.0000	0.8824**	0.8808**
1983-1985	0.8713**	0.8824**	1.0000	0.8529**
1986-1989	0.8512**	0.8808**	0.8529**	1.0000
Interindustry IDK				
1976-1979	0.6852**	0.6653**	0.6684**	0.7455**
1980-1982	0.6729**	0.6277**	0.7115**	0.7121**
1983-1985	0.6811**	0.6140**	0.6696**	0.7102**
1986-1989	0.6556**	0.6063**	0.6667**	0.6791**

Table 5.8-(Continued)

	Interindustry IDK 1976-1979	Interindustry IDK 1980-1982	Interindustry IDK 1983-1985	Interindustry IDK 1986-1989
Innovation Potential	0.7325**	0.7391**	0.7418**	0.7332**
Urbanization Economies	0.7485**	0.7332**	0.7147**	0.7335**
Localization Economies	0.5206**	0.4935**	0.4965**	0.4630**
Federal Govt. Demand-Pull	0.4034**	0.3912**	0.3970**	0.3904**
College Educated	0.4355**	0.4267**	0.4741**	0.5344**
Graduate Degree	0.5402**	0.5491**	0.5154**	0.5255**
Ph.D. in Mech. Eng.	-0.0786	0.0663	-0.0083	0.0875
Industrial Restructuring	0.2106	0.1601	0.1152	0.0903
IT Investment	0.7451**	0.7023**	0.7219**	0.7154**
Intraindustry IDK				
1976-1979	0.6852**	0.6729**	0.6811**	0.6556**
1980-1982	0.6643**	0.6277**	0.6140**	0.6063**
1983-1985	0.6684**	0.7115**	0.6696**	0.6667**
1986-1989	0.7455**	0.7121**	0.7102**	0.6791**
Interindustry IDK				
1976-1979	1.0000	0.9084**	0.9188/**	0.8800**
1980-1982	0.9084**	1.0000	0.9063**	0.8947**
1983-1985	0.9188**	0.9063**	1.0000	0.9346**
1986-1989	0.8800**	0.8947**	0.9346**	1.0000

*=significance at the 5% level
**=significance at the 1% level

Table 5.9-Results of excluding IT investment

Dependent Variable: Machine Tool Innovation Potential

Variable	**Coefficient**
Intercept	-8.337
	(-2.558*)
Agglomeration Economies	
Urbanization Economies (ln)	0.511
	(2.397*)
Localization Economies (ln)	0.255
	(2.594*)
Federal Government Demand-Pull	-0.024
	(-0.220)
Human Capital	
College Educated (ln)	1.224
	(1.039)
Graduate Degree (ln)	-0.287
	(-0.352)
Ph.D. Graduates in Mechanical	0.328
Engineering Produced Locally (ln)	(2.030)
Industrial Restructuring	
Shift to Services (ln)	-0.051
	(-0.276)
Adjusted R^2	0.517
df	31

*=significance at the 5% level

**=significance at the 1% level

Numbers in parentheses are t-scores.

Table 5.10-Results of separating the human capital variables

Dependent Variable: Machine Tool Innovation Potential

Variable	Model 1	Model 2	Model 3
Intercept	-9.995	-8.365	-8.356
	(-4.195**)	(-4.212**)	(-4.525)
Agglomeration Economies			
Urbanization Economies (ln)	0.344	0.201	0.196
	(1.374)	(0.666)	(0.706)
Localization Economies (ln)	0.164	0.230	0.095
	(1.868)	(2.440*)	(1.209)
Federal Government Demand-Pull (ln)	0.010	-0.004	-0.001
	(0.130)	(-0.041)	(-0.014)
Human Capital			
College Educated (ln)	0.575	-	-
	(0.855)		
Graduate Degree (ln)	-	0.799	-
		(1.636)	
Ph.D. Grads. in Mechanical Eng. Produced Locally (ln)	-	-	0.261
			(2.063*)
Industrial Restructuring			
Shift to Services (ln)	0.055	0.003	0.059
	(0.393)	(0.017)	(0.376)
IT Investment (ln)	0.291	0.301	0.630
	(1.249)	(1.027)	(2.777**)
Adjusted R^2	0.585	0.529	0.665
df	54	44	38

*=significance at the 5% level

**=significance at the 1% level

Numbers in parentheses are t-scores

84

Table 5.11-Results of breaking the correlation between urbanization economies and IT investment by omitting urbanization economies

Dependent Variable: Machine Tool Innovation Potential

Variable	Model 1	Model 2	Model 3
Intercept	-8.251 (-4.055**)	-7.697 (-4.522**)	-7.621 (-5.035**)
Agglomeration Economies			
Localization Economies (ln)	0.150 (1.706)	0.222 (2.394*)	0.092 (1.189)
Federal Government Demand-Pull (ln)	0.033 (0.443)	0.009 (0.107)	0.009 (0.113)
Human Capital			
College Educated (ln)	0.441 (0.657)	-	-
Graduate Degree (ln)	-	0.761 (1.580)	-
Ph.D. Grads. in Mechanical Eng. Produced Locally (ln)	-	-	0.232 (1.953)
Industrial Restructuring			
Shift to Services (ln)	0.082 (0.592)	0.022 (0.146)	0.080 (0.527)
IT Investment (ln)	0.551 (3.989**)	0.465 (2.945**)	0.764 (6.206**)
Adjusted R^2	0.577	0.535	0.670
df	54	44	38

*=significance at the 5% level
**=significance at the 1% level
Numbers in parentheses are t-scores

college educated and the graduate degree variables with a Pearson correlation coefficient of 0.8384. The only other correlation of significance among these variables is that between the graduate degree variable and the Ph.D. variable. The correlation coefficient between these two variables is only 0.3288, but it is significant at the 5% level. Therefore, there is ample justification to separate these variables and run three separate models as shown in table 5.12.[3]

Factors Influencing the Development of the Innovation Potential of the Machine Tool Industry

Agglomeration Economies

The results of the final calibrations of the model for the machine tool industry are given in models one, two, and three of table 5.12.[4] Of the two types of agglomeration economies, urbanization economies have a greater impact on the regional innovation potential of the machine tool industry than do localization economies, although both are highly significant. Thus, both an agglomeration of general economic resources and an agglomeration of firms within the same industry are important factors, but urbanization economies have an elasticity ranging from 0.460 to 0.841 while localization economies have an elasticity ranging from 0.143 to 0.266. Put another way, urbanization economies appear to have an impact approximately two to five times greater than that of localization economies.

One possible explanation as to why urbanization economies appear to have a more significant impact on the development of the innovation potential of the machine tool industry is that the machine tool producers need to be close to their customers. As the supplier of the capital goods to the manufacturing sector, the machine tool industry is critical to a wide variety of industries. Thus, they interface locally with a number of customers from different industries, and as described in the chain-linked model of innovation

---

[3] Tables D.1 and D.2 in appendix D show the metro-regions included in each of the models.

[4] In an attempt to capture any non-linear effects of agglomeration economies, the square of both urbanization $[(\ln(UE))^2]$ and localization $[(\ln(LE))^2]$ economies were entered into the model. The correlation between $\ln(UE)$ and $(\ln(UE))^2$ is 0.9992, and the correlation between $\ln(LE)$ and $(\ln(LE))^2$ is 0.9950. Since the variables were almost perfectly collinear, no substantive results were derived from these models.

Table 5.12-Factors influencing innovation potential

Dependent Variable: Machine Tool Innovation Potential

Variable	Model 1	Model 2	Model 3
Intercept	-11.185	-8.559	-8.911
	(-5.092**)	(-4.328**)	(-4.425**)
Agglomeration Economies			
Urbanization Economies (ln)	0.596	0.460	0.841
	(4.042**)	(2.815**)	(5.052**)
Localization Economies (ln)	0.207	0.266	0.143
	(2.558*)	(3.050**)	(1.712)
Federal Government Demand-Pull (ln)	0.0003	-0.022	0.005
	(0.004)	(-0.257)	(0.059)
Human Capital			
College Educated (ln)	0.956	-	-
	(1.585)		
Graduate Degree (ln)	-	0.986	-
		(2.174*)	
Ph.D. Grads. in Mechanical Eng. Produced Locally (ln)	-	-	0.320
			(2.338*)
Industrial Restructuring			
Shift to Services (ln)	0.026	-0.027	-0.082
	(0.190)	(-0.172)	(-0.506)
Adjusted R^2	0.580	0.528	0.597
df	54	44	38

*=significance at the 5% level
**=significance at the 1% level
Numbers in parentheses are t-scores

Table 5.12-(Continued)

Dependent Variable: Semiconductor Innovation Potential

Variable	Model 4	Model 5	Model 6
Intercept	-14.808 (-3.838**)	-11.767 (-3.713**)	-8.272 (-3.558**)
Agglomeration Economies			
Urbanization Economies (ln)	0.443 (1.647)	0.387 (1.276)	0.632 (2.631*)
Localization Economies (ln)	0.482 (2.956**)	0.504 (3.021**)	0.513 (3.502**)
Federal Government Demand-Pull (ln)	0.033 (0.309)	0.031 (0.281)	-0.057 (-0.599)
Human Capital			
College Educated (ln)	1.806 (1.797)	-	-
Graduate Degree (ln)	-	1.589 (2.438*)	-
Ph.D. Grads. in Electrical Eng. Produced Locally (ln)	-	-	0.655 (3.632**)
Industrial Restructuring			
Shift to Services (ln)	-0.011 (-0.048)	-0.046 (-0.178)	0.014 (0.075)
Adjusted R^2	0.582	0.588	0.677
df	38	34	32

*=significance at the 5% level
**=significance at the 1% level
Numbers in parentheses are t-scores

(Kline and Rosenberg, 1986), it is important for them to obtain feedback from these customers. This can be a vital source of input into their innovative process because their customers can tell them what needs to be changed or added to the machines to make them better: being close to their customers provides opportunities for the exchange of ideas and experience that might not otherwise occur (Kaldor, 1970). Experience gained by working with the customer before, during, and after the installation process in an operating factory can provide vital pieces of information leading to future inventions and innovations. This is similar to the benefits derived from the process of "learning by using" as defined by Rosenberg (1982).

In model three, the coefficient on the urbanization economies variable almost doubles relative to its size in models one and two. This could be explained by the movement from a more general definition of human capital to a more narrowly defined measure. The human capital variable in model three is locally-produced Ph.D. graduates in mechanical engineering, which is a more narrowly defined measure than the college educated or graduate degree variables. Thus, the urbanization economies variable in model three may be capturing some of the effects captured by the college educated and graduate degree variables in models one and two, respectively. Because the college educated and graduate degree variables in models one and two, respectively, include workers with a variety of educational backgrounds, they capture a more general pool of skilled labor and educational resources than does the Ph.D. variable found in model three. It is the more general measures of skilled labor and educational resources not captured by the Ph.D. variable that may be spilling over into the urbanization economies variable in model three.

There is a significant correlation between urbanization and localization economies. Thus, models were run with these variables separated in order to provide some insight into potential problems. These results are shown in table 5.13, and indicate that the variables maintain their significance even when the correlation between the two is broken. In either the case of table 5.12 or table 5.13, the results appear to be the same. It appears, then, that multicollinearity is not a problem in this case. The common variation of the two variables has no substantive effect on the results.

89

Table 5.13-Results of separating localization and urbanization economies

Dependent Variable: Machine Tool Innovation Potential

Variable	Model 1	Model 2	Model 3
Intercept	-9.550 (-4.311**)	-8.229 (-3.792**)	-13.503 (-4.737**)
Agglomeration Economies			
Urbanization Economies (ln)	0.740 (5.149**)	0.654 (3.946**)	0.918 (5.572**)
Localization Economies (ln)	-	-	-
Federal Government Demand-Pull (ln)	0.101 (1.463)	0.123 (1.554)	0.076 (0.891)
Human Capital			
College Educated (ln)	0.314 (0.543)	-	-
Graduate Degree (ln)	-	0.438 (0.956)	-
Ph.D. Grads. in Mechanical Eng. Produced Locally (ln)	-	-	0.335 (2.391*)
Industrial Restructuring			
Shift to Services (ln)	0.024 (0.165)	-0.001 (-0.008)	-0.049 (-0.297)
Adjusted R^2	0.533	0.430	0.574
df	54	44	38

*=significance at the 5% level
**=significance at the 1% level
Numbers in parentheses are t-scores

Table 5.13-(Continued)

Dependent Variable: Machine Tool Innovation Potential

Variable	Model 4	Model 5	Model 6
Intercept	-7.735	-4.180	-1.170
	(-3.343**)	(-3.157**)	(-0.646)
Agglomeration Economies			
Urbanization Economies (ln)	-	-	-
Localization Economies (ln)	0.332	0.361	0.257
	(3.878**)	(4.147**)	(2.436*)
Federal Government Demand-Pull (ln)	0.075	-0.002	0.177
	(0.883)	(-0.018)	(1.558)
Human Capital			
College Educated (ln)	1.989	-	-
	(3.186**)		
Graduate Degree (ln)	-	1.480	-
		(3.264**)	
Ph.D. Grads. in Mechanical Eng. Produced Locally (ln)	-	-	0.081
			(0.480)
Industrial Restructuring			
Shift to Services (ln)	0.037	0.003	-0.205
	(0.235)	(0.020)	(-0.975)
Adjusted R^2	0.451	0.446	0.306
df	54	44	38

*=significance at the 5% level
**=significance at the 1% level
Numbers in parentheses are t-scores

As expected, human capital plays a significant role as facilitator of machine tool invention. Of the three categories of human capital, only the percentage of those who are college educated is insignificant. From these results, those regions with a higher percentage of people with a graduate degree are going to be the most conducive to machine tool invention, with an elasticity three times greater than the measure of mechanical engineering Ph.D. graduates. Overall, these results support the hypothesis that those regions with a larger pool of highly educated workers are best able to spawn invention, as well as attract the most inventive firms (Suarez-Villa, 1993; Suarez-Villa and Hasnath, 1993).

The significance of the graduate degree and Ph.D. variables combined with the insignificance of the college educated variable indicates that there is some discounting of college educated labor by the economy. In other words, industry needs the higher-order skills produced in a graduate program, and it needs to be close to knowledge creation and its application in order to facilitate innovation. Furthermore, this shows that in order to technologically advance an industry, there needs to be a stock of highly skilled labor from which the industry can draw.

What would explain the lesser impact of the Ph.D. variable relative to the graduate degree variable? One possible explanation is derived from the difference between the masters and doctorate degrees. The masters degree is generally pursued by those who have aspirations to work in industry, and the training received at this level places more emphasis on invention in the process of product development for industry. The Ph.D. degree, on the other hand, is generally a more academic degree, with the emphasis placed more on theoretical work. Those who hold doctorate degrees are more likely to work in an academic setting pursuing fundamental inquiry for the sake of the advancement of knowledge. Thus, the work of those who earn a Ph.D. does not stress invention relative to the work of those with a masters degree, but as Feldman (1992), Jaffe (1989), Mansfield (1991), and Nelson (1982) argue, university research does lead to some patents and does contribute significantly to the innovative process. The upshot is that although those with a Ph.D. in mechanical or electrical engineering may not produce patents as proficiently as the pool of labor holding a graduate degree, the results of this study confirm the arguments put forth by others that they still make a significant contribution to the development of the region's innovation potential.

Two other explanations also are possible. The first deals with the sheer size of the stocks of these types of labor. The stock of labor with a graduate degree is larger than the stock of labor with a Ph.D. produced from a local institution. Thus, the stock of those with a graduate degree will register a larger impact just from its larger size. Secondly, since the graduate degree variable includes a broad array of degrees, it captures, to some extent, the synergy across disciplines involved in the development of innovation potential. For example, as Kline and Rosenberg (1986) put forth in their chain-linked model of innovation, feedback from marketing and finance, for instance, are vital to the innovative process. The graduate degree variable captures the role of those highly skilled in those areas outside of science and engineering that provide important feedback to the scientists and engineers directly involved in the R&D process. In other words, it is a broader measure allowing it to register a larger impact.

Referring back to table 5.13, some interesting findings regarding the human capital variables resulted from splitting agglomeration economies into separate models. In models one through three of table 5.13, the college educated variable is still not significant and the graduate degree variable loses significance relative to model two in table 5.12. These two variables are significant in models four and five where the urbanization economies variable is dropped, indicating that they are capturing the effects of urbanization economies (further evidence is provided by the significant correlations between college educated and graduate degree with urbanization economies - see correlation tables). When both urbanization and localization economies are included, the college educated variable loses its significance, and the impact of the graduate degree variable is decreased. This indicates that the urbanization economies variable is capturing some of the effects of these variables, but combined with results from models four and five in table 5.13, we can say that having a well-educated labor force (i.e. bachelor's degree or higher) matters in developing regional innovation potential.

Moving to the Ph.D. variable, we see in model three in table 5.13 that it is significant, as it is in model three of table 5.12. Since the Ph.D. variable is an industry-specific measure in this study, it appears that it is capturing the effect of localization economies in model three of table 5.13, since the localization economies variable is a measure of the industry's agglomeration of resources. It is also instructive to note that the magnitude of the coefficient on the Ph.D. variable in model three of table 5.13 is not much different than it is in model three of table 5.12. Furthermore, localization economies in model three of table 5.12 are insignificant. These results appear to indicate that having Ph.D.s in mechanical engineering is the main resource comprising localization economies.

Local doctoral-degree granting graduate programs   These human capital variables also measure, to a certain extent, the value of having universities present within the region both as a source of invention and as a source of human capital. The Ph.D. variable gets the closest to capturing this effect since it actually measures the doctorates in mechanical engineering produced by universities within the region. Since it also captures the presence of a Ph.D. program where research may be occurring, it will also yield a sense of the impact of universities as a source of invention. This is not to completely downplay the college educated and graduate degree variables. However, since these are not region-specific measures, it is highly likely that a good number of these people were educated in other regions. While numerous of these people were probably educated within the region, these variables do not provide as clean a regional measure of human capital and patent production by local universities. Either way, the significance of the Ph.D. measure indicates that the presence of a university with a doctoral-degree granting graduate program within the region facilitates invention to a significant extent.

Federal Government Demand-Pull

The remaining two categories of variables - federal government demand-pull and industrial restructuring - are insignificant in all models. A possible explanation as to why machine tool procurement by the federal government does not register a significant demand-pull impact is that it accounts for a very small percentage of total regional machine tool output. As a percent of regional machine tool output, federal government procurement ranged from 0.04% to 24.60%, but the average was only 1.58% indicating that the machine tool output within most regions was produced to satisfy demand from sectors other than the federal government. In other words, the demand for machine tools was too small to register a demand-pull effect.

94

Furthermore, American science and technology has largely been implemented through the space and defense programs with little impact on the commercial sector (Hicks and Lee 1994).

> American policy is less explicitly interventionist, and has long held that government procurement for military and space programmes is a superior method of reaping the benefits of high technology.[5] This policy has recently been called into question, both because of the reduced potential for commercialization of military technology, and because of diminished concerns about military threats in comparison to economic ones.[6] In addition, there is growing concern that 'the pattern of indirect commercial or economic benefits – spinoffs – is no longer providing the United States with enough technologies that are competitive in the international marketplace' (Kash 1989: 37). However, dependence on Defense Department funding has continued, for both software development and for advanced semiconductor manufacturing techniques (SEMATECH), and generally characterizes the US approach to S&T [science and technology] policy.[7] Beyond military demand pull, US S&T policy is only indirect and implicit, working through the regulatory and tax systems[8] (Malecki, 1991, pp.272-273).

Much of the demand-pull effect from the federal government, therefore, has been expressed through the procurement of military items, with little impact on the innovation potential of the private commercial sector. As the results indicate, this appears to be the case for the innovation potential of the machine tool industry.

Shift to Services

The shift to services does not have a significant impact on the inventive level of the machine tool industry at the metro-regional level. It is hard to say whether this is welcome news for the machine tool industry, since it can be argued that this restructuring can either enhance or stifle the inventive abilities of this industry. The relative decline of manufacturing will lessen the demand-

---

[5] As cited in Malecki (1991), see also Abernathy and Chakravarthy (1979); Allen et al. (1978); Levin (1982); Molina (1989); Nelson (1982, 1984); Roessner (1987).

[6] As cited in Malecki (1991), see also Neff, Magnusson, and Holstein (1989).

[7] As cited in Malecki (1991), see also Borrus (1988); Flamm (1987); Foray, Gibbons and Ferne (1989).

[8] As cited in Malecki (1991), see also Bean and Baker (1988); Rees (1987); Rothwell (1980).

pull influence causing a decline in machine tool invention, but on the other hand, the shift to services requires the manufacture of new types of equipment which will require new machine tools to bend, shape, or cut metal in different ways. This latter scenario should enhance machine tool invention. Since there is some indication that this shift has not led to a significant effect, one could argue the impacts are at least not deleterious to the industry.

Invention-Derived Knowledge

It has been argued that past inventive activity influences present inventive activity in two ways. First, such activity provides the technological foundation requisite to pursuing certain inventions. In other words, past inventions provide the technology that make it possible to create certain inventions. Second, it provides the inventor with new ideas and directs him or her toward new opportunities they might not have seen had the past invention not been created.

These impacts can be felt through both intraindustry and interindustry inventive activity. That is, not only can inventions in the machine tool industry influence future inventive activity in the machine tool industry, but inventions in other industries may also impact the machine tool industry in a similar manner. This begs two questions. One, what is the lag structure of such impacts both within and across industries, and two, is the lag structure different within and across industries?

Intraindustry effects   In order to capture the effects of past inventions within the same industry, simple bivariate Pearson correlation coefficients between the natural log of innovation potential and the natural log of machine tool patents lagged over four time periods were calculated. These time periods correspond with the periodic shifts of the business cycle and thus, control for whatever impact the business cycle would have on inventive activities. The 1976-1979 was a period of stagflation; the 1980-1982 period was a recessionary period; the 1983-1985 period was one of rapid growth; and 1986-1989 was a period of slowing growth leading into a recession.

As illustrated in top panel of table 5.14, the most recent lagged time period (1986-1989) has the highest correlation as expected. Within the machine tool industry, though, the second highest correlation is in the earliest time period (1976-1979). From there, the correlations decrease to

96

their lowest point in the 1980-1982 period and then increase to the highest one of 0.8667 in the 1986-1989 period. In other words, the lag structure is somewhat parabolic (see figure 5.2).

Table 5.14-Pearson correlation coefficients between innovation potential and past inventive activity

Machine Tool Innovation Potential vs. Machine Tool Patents

1976-1979 = 0.8392
1980-1982 = 0.7782
1983-1985 = 0.8248
1986-1989 = 0.8667

Machine Tool Innovation Potential vs. Semiconductor Patents

1976-1979 = 0.7325
1980-1982 = 0.7391
1983-1985 = 0.7418
1986-1989 = 0.7332

Semiconductor Innovation Potential vs. Semiconductor Patents

1976-1979 = 0.7541
1980-1982 = 0.8253
1983-1985 = 0.8198
1986-1989 = 0.9123

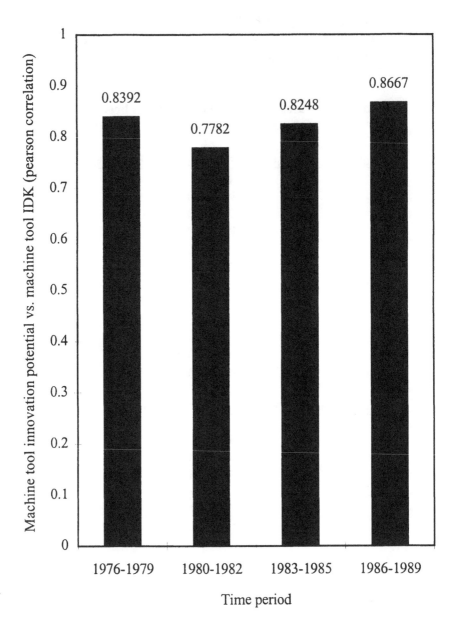

Figure 5.2 Effects of machine tool intraindustry invention-derived knowledge transfer (correlation results)

The parabolic lag structure can possibly be explained by the fact that 1980-1982 was a severe recessionary period, causing a squeeze on research and development resources as firms attempt to lower costs in order to survive a combinaton of rapid inflation and slow growth. It seems plausible to expect a decline in inventive activity during such a time period, especially in a cyclical industry like machine tools. Such a decline would lead to the lower correlation coefficient seen in the table.

Interindustry effects   In order to analyze the impact of patenting activity across industries, the natural log of semiconductor patents over the four time periods was correlated with the machine tool innovation potential. Previous research has shown that the transmission across industries has a longer lag than within industries (Beggs, 1984), and this is what we find with the transmission from the semiconductor industry to the machine tool industry. For example, semiconductor patents granted during the 1983-1985 time period have the largest impact on machine tool inventive activity during 1990-1992 (see table 5.14 and figure 5.3), but within the same industry, patents granted during the 1986-1989 period had the largest impact. Thus, we find support for the hypothesis that the transmission of ideas across industries has a longer lag time than within the same industry.

OLS results   As discussed earlier, OLS regressions were run with only one time period of invention-derived knowledge variables included in the models in order to break the correlations among these variables. The results from these models (the coefficients on these variables are reproduced from tables 5.2-5.5 to table 5.15) are similar to those from the simple bivariate Pearson correlations.

For example, the average of the intraindustry coefficients gives a parabolic lag structure as shown in figure 5.4. The average effects of the transfer of such knowledge within the same industry are slightly smaller in the regression models relative to the correlations.

The average effects of the interindustry transfer of this knowledge in the regressions (see table 5.15 and figure 5.5) also show a similar lag structure as the correlation results did with the 1983-1985 and the 1980-1982 periods having the greatest impact on machine tool innovation potential. Once again, this provides evidence that the transfer of knowledge embodied in patents between industries has a longer lag than within industries. Unlike the interindustry effects shown by the correlations, the average interindustry effects of the regressions are considerably smaller than

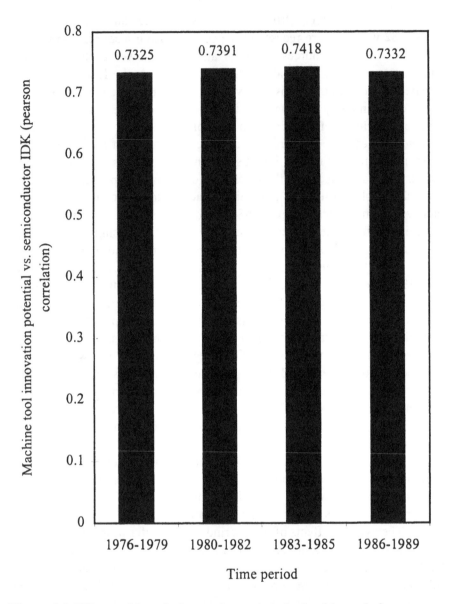

Figure 5.3 Effects of interindustry invention-derived knowledge transfer (correlation results)

the intraindustry effects, indicating that while patents related to other industries have a significant impact on the development of innovation potential within another industry, that impact is considerably weaker.

Table 5.15-Coefficients on IDK variables

Intraindustry Knowledge Transfer

Time Period	Model 1	Model 2	Model 3	Average
1976-1979	0.600	0.607	0.512	0.573
1980-1982	0.477	0.656	0.512	0.548
1983-1985	0.543	0.607	0.746	0.632
1986-1989	0.791	0.862	0.826	0.826

Interindustry Knowledge Transfer

Time Period	Model 4	Model 5	Model 6	Average
1976-1979	0.134	0.174	0.138	0.149
1980-1982	0.236	0.306	0.187	0.243
1983-1985	0.230	0.237	0.261	0.243
1986-1989	0.234	0.244	0.200	0.226

NOTE: The numbers in this table were transferred from the models in tables 5.2-5.5.

Information Technology Investment Revisited

Through a process of backward stepwise elimination, variables were eliminated from the model in table 5.7 one at a time until arriving at the model shown in table 5.16. Model one in table 5.16 is the same as model three in

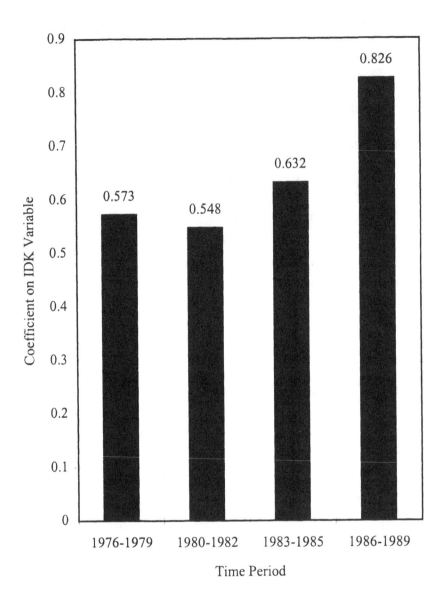

Figure 5.4 Effects of intraindustry invention-derived knowledge transfer (OLS results)

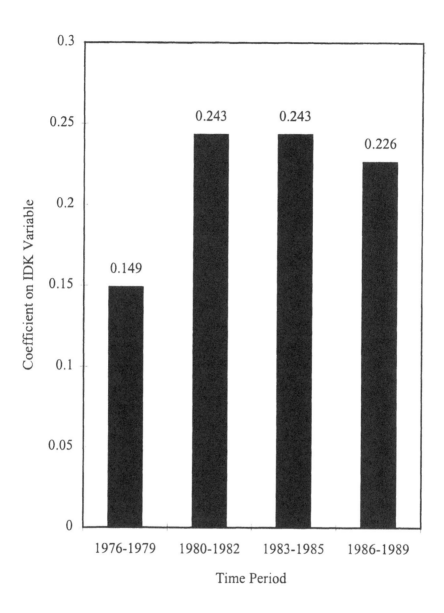

Figure 5.5 Effects of interindustry invention-derived knowledge transfer (OLS results)

table 5.10, except federal government demand-pull and industrial restructuring are excluded. In essence, by omitting these two variables, some of the multicollinearity problems associated with the IT investment variable discussed earlier have been removed. However, the high correlation between IT investment and urbanization economies appears to eliminate the significant effect of urbanization economies at the 1% level, as shown in model three of table 5.12, although urbanization economies is significant at the 10% level in table 5.16. These results suggest that investment in information technology is a catalyst for the development of metro-regional machine tool innovation potential.

Do the Impacts of the Metro-Regional Determinants of Innovation Potential Vary Across Industries?

In an attempt to gain some insight into the applicability of these regional influences across industries, the same models were run for the semiconductor industry. The results are shown in models four, five, and six of table 5.12.

The biggest difference between the two industries is the impact that agglomeration economies have on their respective regional innovation potential. As mentioned earlier, urbanization economies have a larger impact than do localization economies in the machine tool industry while just the opposite is true for the semiconductor industry. Also, the difference in relative importance between the two types is even more dramatic in the semiconductor industry. For example, in models four and five, urbanization economies are not significant. They are only significant in model six. The explanation for the large increase in this variable in model six is the same as that given for the increase in the size of the coefficient in model three. That is, the urbanization economies variable is capturing the effect of the general pool of skilled labor and the broad educational infrastructure captured by the human capital variables in models four and five but not in model six. Comparing similar models where this variable is significant - i.e., models three and six - we see that urbanization economies have a greater elasticity (0.841) and are more statistically significant in the machine tool industry than in the semiconductor industry (0.632).

The opposite relationship between the two industries holds for localization economies. Within the semiconductor industry, it is more

104

Table 5.16 Results of backward stepwise regression: IT investment revisited

Dep Var: Machine Tool Innovation Potential Variable	Model 1	Dep Var: Semiconductor Innovation Potential Model 2
Intercept	-9.483 (-6.110**)	-10.014 (-4.367**)
Agglomeration Economies		
Urbanization Economies (ln)	0.437 (1.842)	0.377 (0.953)
Localization Economies (ln)	0.133 (2.102*)	0.475 (4.029**)
Ph.D. Grads. in Mechanical Eng. Produced Locally (ln)	0.241 (2.192*)	
Ph.D. Grads. in Electrical Emg. Produced Locally (ln)		0.466 (2.907**)
IT Investment (ln)	0.424 (2.167*)	0.324 (0.987)
Adjusted R^2	0.676	0.644
df	45	47

*=significance at the 5% level
**=significance at the 1% level
Numbers in parentheses are t-scores

important to be located within agglomerations of firms of the same industry than it is for firms in the machine tool industry. The elasticities for models four through six are approximately 2 to 3.5 times larger than those in models one through three, but the significance levels are more in line with each other, though. One possible explanation for this difference is that the firms within the semiconductor industry may need to be closer to their competitors, given the more rapid pace of technological change occurring within this industry.[9] This allows them the opportunity to keep close watch on their competition, which enables them to move more quickly and maintain the pace in the technological race. It also provides them the opportunity to cross-pollinate ideas among workers within the industry. In an industry that advances quickly, the mixing of workers across the industry could be an invaluable source of ideas allowing for some firms to gain a competitive advantage. This is true for any industry, but it is especially true in an industry that advances technology at a very fast pace.

The other set of variables that makes for an instructive comparison is the human capital variables. As is the case with the development of machine tool innovation potential, those regions with a larger stock of labor holding graduate degrees are going to be the best hosts of the development of semiconductor innovation potential. There is also evidence of discounting of college educated labor with respect to semiconductor innovation potential. For the semiconductor industry (as is somewhat true for the machine tool industry), we see a progressive decrease in the elasticity as we move to a more narrow definition, attaining higher levels of education. For instance, the elasticity on percent college educated is 1.806, 1.589 for percent with a graduate degree, and the percent with a Ph.D. in mechanical engineering is the most inelastic at 0.655.

Comparing across industries, all of the human capital variables have an elasticity approximately twice as great in models four through six as they do in models one through three. Also, all of these variables are inelastic in the machine tool industry while both percent with a college degree and graduate degree are elastic in the semiconductor models. These results indicate that a plentiful stock of well-educated human capital is important to the inventive processes of both industries, but it is approximately twice as important to the newer of the two, the semiconductor industry.

As with the machine tool industry, the demand-pull from the government and the restructuring of the economy (i.e., shift to services) had no significant impact on the innovation potential of the semiconductor industry. As was the case in the machine tool industry, the lack of an impact from the

---

[9] As evidence of the more rapid pace of technological change in the semiconductor industry, there were 14,056 semiconductor patents of U.S. origin granted from 1980 through 1989 (source: U.S Patent and Trademark Office). During the same time period, there were 5,692 machine tool patents of U.S. origin granted (source: U.S. Patent and Trademark Office).

demand of the federal government could be due to the fact that average annual federal government semiconductor procurement was only 0.509% of average annual semiconductor output on average.

The sectoral restructuring of the economy had no impact on the inventive level of semiconductors, just as was the case in the machine tool industry. It seems reasonable to expect that as business services grow, the demand for machines that use semiconductors, such as computers, would grow with it. This increased demand could possibly have a demand-pull effect, but at the regional level, no significant effect is found.

Unlike the machine tool industry, the innovation potential of the semiconductor industry is not significantly influenced by information technology investment, as shown in model two of table 5.16. This is possibly due to the differences in the structures of the two industries. The semiconductor industry consists of a greater number of large firms relative to the machine tool industry, where small firms are still predominant. Thus, the flow of information across computer networks may be more important to machine tool firms because the smaller firms in this industry necessarily have to extend outside of their firm for the information that drives innovation. On the other hand, the larger firms comprising the semiconductor industry have a substantial internal flow of innovation-relevant information, which lessens their need to acquire information external to the firm over computer networks.

The final comparison is that of the lag structure of intraindustry transfer invention derived knowledge. Within the semiconductor industry, the effect of IDK on innovation potential has a similar lag structure to that of the machine tool industry. As shown in the bottom panel of table 5.14, the most recent time period (1986-1989) had the largest influence on innovation potential, just as was the case with machine tool innovation potential. For semiconductors, the lag structure across all four time periods was more linear, with the 1976-1979 IDK having the smallest impact (see figure 5.6). Thus, it appears that the transfer of invention derived knowledge within the same industry has a similar lag structure, regardless of the industry.

107

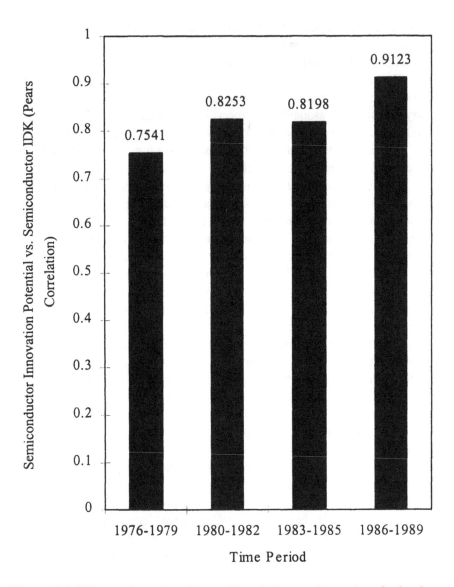

Figure 5.6 Effects of semiconductor intraindustry invention-derived knowledge transfer (correlation results)

6 Summary and Implications

Summary

This study was undertaken with two goals in mind: to describe the geographic landscape of the innovation potential of machine tools and to discover those metro-regional inputs or endowments that play key roles in the development of this innovation potential. In addition, a third goal was to analyze these influences across industries. To provide some perspective, the study began with a historical look at the technological development of the machine tool industry from its very beginnings to the present.

The history of the machine tool industry from a technological perspective illustrated that many of the variables used in this study likely have been exerting an influence on the development of the machine tool industry since its birth. The presence of skilled labor and a demand-pull from the market provided an impetus for the growth of independent machinery producing firms during the mid-1800s. The government's demand for weapons with interchangeable parts was a catalyst for the development of the milling machine and machine tools that were lighter, more specialized, and higher-speed. The demand-pull influences from the automobile, sewing machine, and bicycle industries were also vital to the technological development of machine tools.

Throughout its history, interindustry invention-derived knowledge also played a key role in the technological development of machine tools. This is especially true in the case of numerically controlled and computer numerically controlled machine tools. The Jacquard loom was actually the first tool that could be programmed, and it was this technology that was adapted to create the first numerically controlled machine tools. With the creation of the computer, programming machine tools became much easier, allowing for the significant development of computer numerically controlled tools.

Some have argued that one of the many reasons for the waning competitiveness of the U.S. machine tool industry in the 1980s could be attributed to a lack of innovation. There were at least two causes: a shortage of skilled labor and the inability of the industry to attain localization economies.

The limited benefit derived by the industry from federally sponsored R&D did not ameliorate these deficiencies. The technologies developed through support of the federal government were too costly to be used effectively in industry, and R&D dollars flowing to universities were not sufficiently beneficial either because very few programs emphasized technologies for manufacturing processes. Most of the emphasis was placed on product design or theoretical engineering.

History thus teaches us that the birth, growth, decline, and recovery of the United States machine tool industry likely rested heavily on technological advance, and this advance, in turn, upon key underlying forces: skilled labor, market size (demand-pull influences), invention derived knowledge, and localization economies. How have these factors shaped the variations in machine tool innovation potential across metro-regions? Both types of agglomeration economies have significant impacts, with urbanization economies having an effect approximately twice as large as that of localization economies. A highly skilled stock of labor also is an important resource for the development of the innovation potential of this industry. The presence of doctoral-granting programs at research universities was found to be a significant endowment within the region as a producer of both skilled labor and patents. The federal government demand-pull and industrial restructuring measures were found to be insignificant. The results also tepidly suggest that information technology investment significantly influences machine tool innovation potential.

With respect to invention-derived knowledge, it was found that the intraindustry lag was shorter than the interindustry lag, as expected. The intraindustry lag structure for the machine tool innovation potential showed a parabolic structure, with IDK in the most recent time period having the largest impact. The parabola was probably business cycle related. Additionally, the interindustry effects of past semiconductor patenting on machine tool innovation potential had a longer lag structure than the intraindustry effect, with the semiconductor IDK in the 1983-1985 period having the largest impact on machine tool innovation potential.

Similar results emerged from a comparison of the forces driving machine tool and semiconductor innovation potential; resources that facilitate the development of innovation potential for one industry also appear to facilitate it for another industry. There were, of course, differences in detail. For the semiconductor industry, localization economies appear to be more important than urbanization economies, while the opposite is true for the machine tool industry. This suggests that the effect of urbanization and

110

localization economies on the development of innovation potential is industry-dependent. The growth engine for semiconductor innovation potential seems to be a more generally skilled pool of human capital, although the response is still significant for the higher skilled, more industry-specific pool as well, and as with machine tool innovation potential, the local presence of a university with a graduate program is an important regional asset. Thus, the impacts of human capital and university presence appear to be similar across industries, with these inputs being slightly more important to the innovation potential of the semiconductor industry. Federal government demand-pull and the shift to services were insignificant in both cases. IT investment was found to have no significant impact on semiconductor innovation potential.

For the most part, these results are consistent with what history has taught us. The technological history of the machine tool industry has shown us that skilled labor, clusters of firms within this industry, and invention-derived knowledge are important to the industry's technological development and to its growth. Agglomeration economies are important facilitators of innovation potential, but urbanization economies are more influential for the machine tool industry while localization economies appear to be more important for semiconductor innovation potential. A highly skilled and educated labor force is an important catalyst for innovation potential. Universities with advanced degree programs represent a significant endowment in developing localized innovation potential. The transmission of ideas embodied in patents has a shorter intraindustry lag than an interindustry lag.

On the other hand, throughout a good part of its history, federal government demand played a significant role as a catalyst to the invention of new machine tools. This was not true for the period 1990-1992. It certainly seems reasonable to argue that this indicates a change in the importance of the government in the technological development of this industry. The industry was born before many of the complementary technologies that could have supplied a need for machine tools were created. Its birth also occurred before the development of many of the auxiliary industries that catalyzed technological change in the machine tool industry. Thus, the government may have had to plant the seed leading to the birth of this industry before the aforementioned developments, but given the vast industrialization of the U.S. economy, it seems plausible that the role of the government may have lessened.

Policy Implications

With a lessened federal role, what are the lessons for public policy? Since the required ingredients for developing the innovation potential of an industry are somewhat similar across industries, the policy implications for developing a region's innovation potential also are similar. Regions looking to enhance their potential for innovation should pursue policies that nurture the entry of new firms in the industry of interest leading, in general, to a cluster of these firms, allowing them to take advantage of the localization and urbanization economies that are derived from such clusters.

Regions should also build or support the infrastructure that trains and educates its labor pool. This means support should be given to local college or university systems, especially those with graduate programs in engineering. If a region is interested in facilitating the innovation potential of a particular industry, it could work to support or develop an appropriate graduate school of engineering. This does not mean that direct support of the engineering program should be provided while ignoring the general college education provided within the region. The optimal policy would be to provide support to both, if at all possible. Furthermore, provision of a sound education should extend to pre-college levels. This could be one feature of the region that might expand and improve the stock of highly skilled labor within the region by attracting such labor to the region.

Future Research

This study is designed to be the beginning of a series of related studies. The question of the applicability of regional endowments to the development of the innovation potential of different industries is particularly intriguing. A natural extension of this study, therefore, would be to apply the same analysis to different industries.

Another interesting question is whether or not regions can appropriate the returns from the innovation potential they develop. Is innovation potential really an engine of economic growth and development at the metro-regional level? This is a more important question, because if a region is not able to capture the returns from their investment in developing their innovation potential, there is little incentive for them to make such investments.

APPENDIX A

GRAPHICAL TESTS FOR HETEROSKEDASTICITY

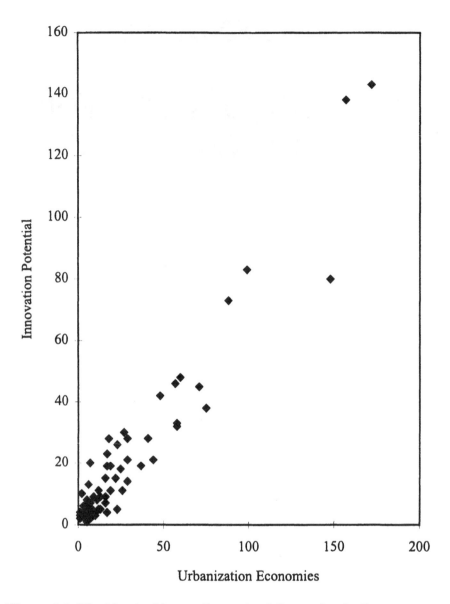

Figure A.1 Machine tool innovation potential vs. urbanization economies

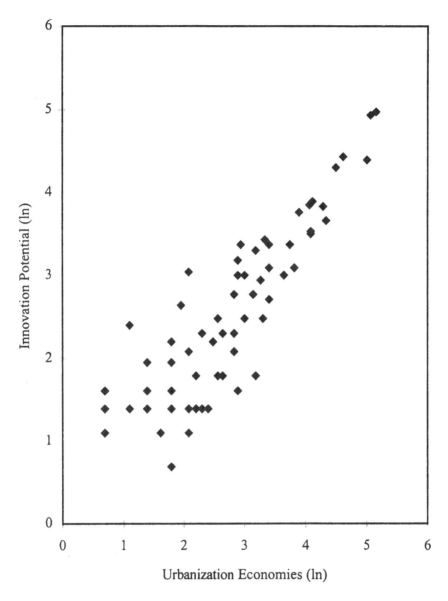

Figure A.2 Machine tool innovation potential (ln) vs. urbanization economies (ln)

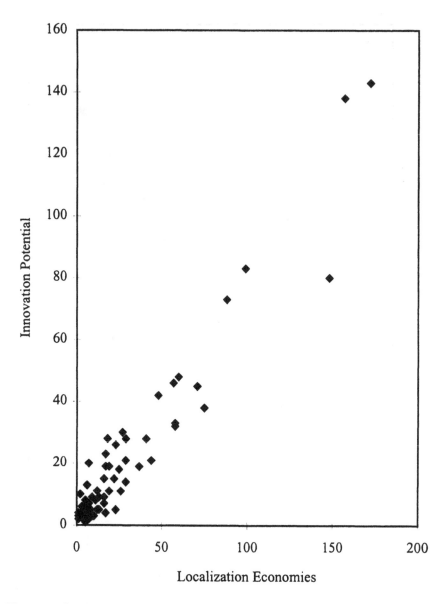

Figure A.3 Machine tool innovation potential vs. localization economies

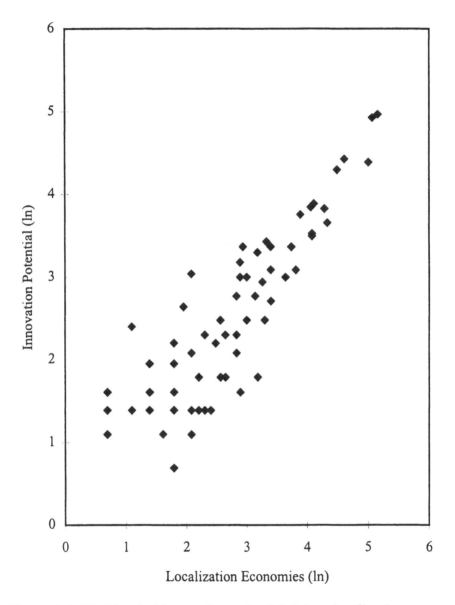

Figure A.4 Machine tool innovation potential (ln) vs. localization economies (ln)

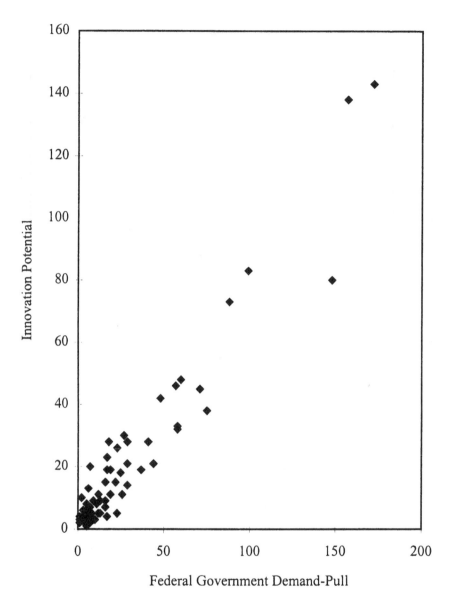

**Figure A.5 Machine tool innovation potential vs. federal government
demand-pull**

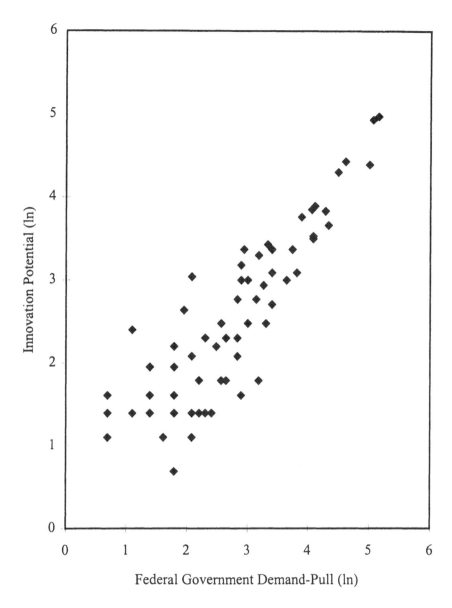

Figure A.6 Machine tool innovation potential (ln) vs. federal government demand-pull (ln)

119

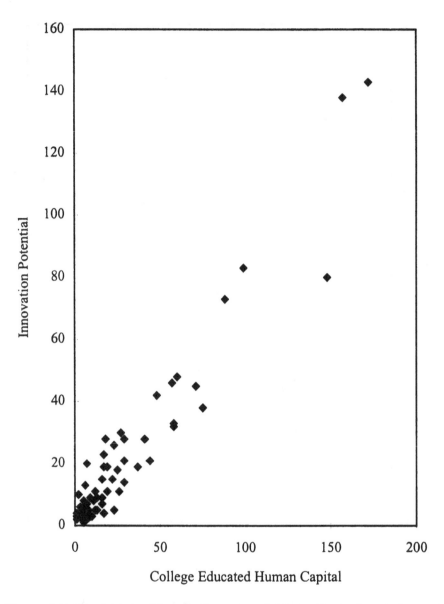

Figure A.7 Machine tool innovation potential vs. college educated human capital

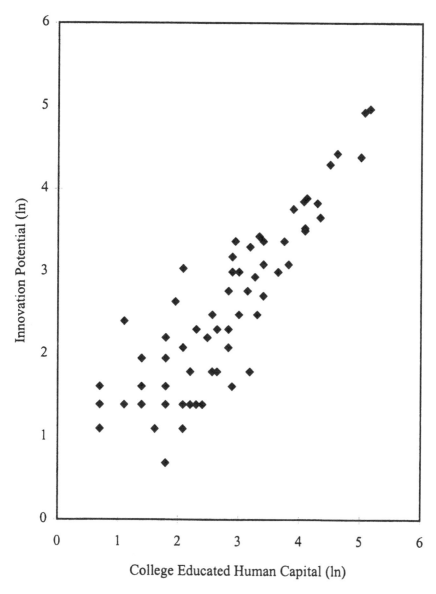

Figure A.8 Machine tool innovation potential (ln) vs. college educated human capital (ln)

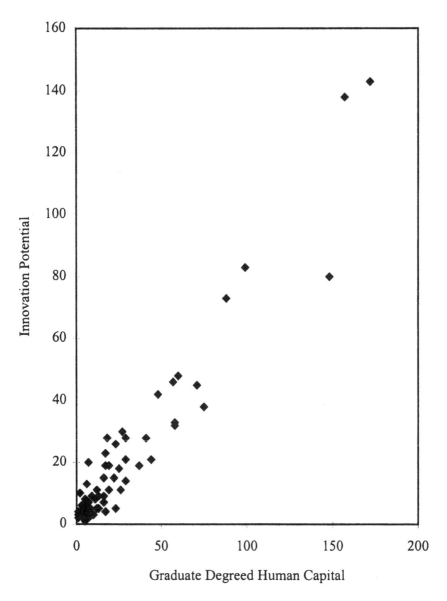

Figure A.9 Machine tool innovation potential vs. graduate degreed human capital

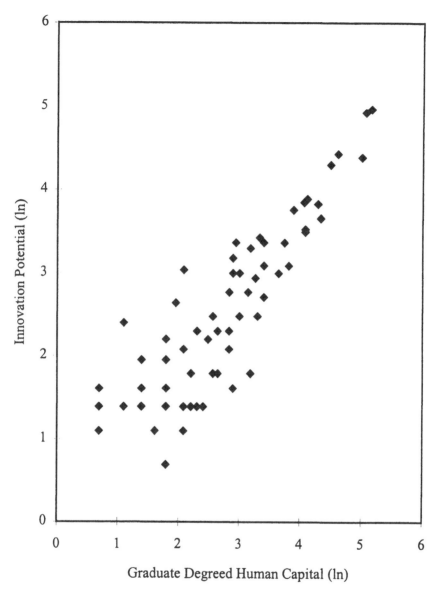

Figure A.10 Machine tool innovation potential (ln) vs. graduate degreed human capital (ln)

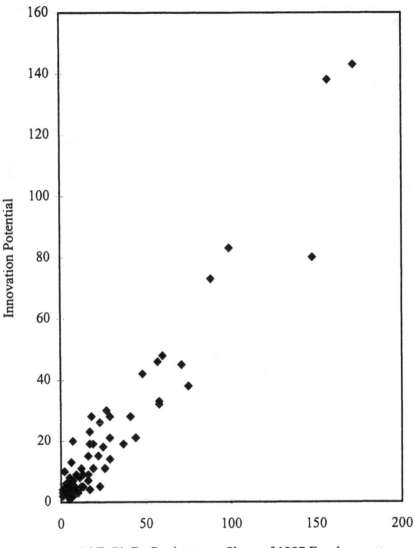

Figure A.11 Machine tool innovation potential vs. mechanical engineering Ph.D. graduates

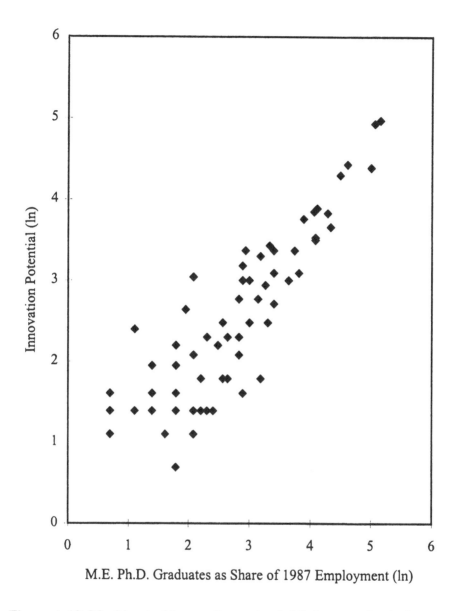

Figure A.12 Machine tool innovation potential (ln) vs. mechanical engineering Ph.D. graduates (ln)

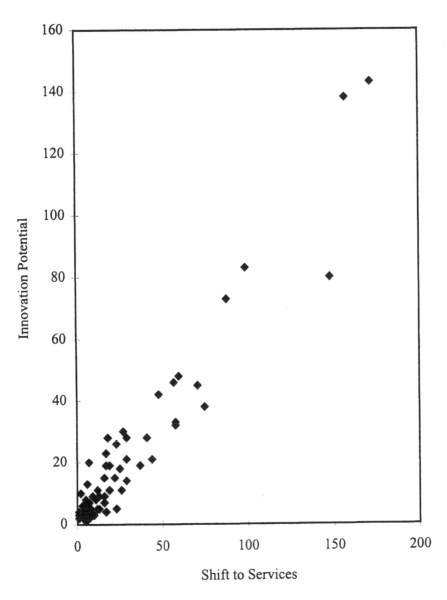

Figure A.13 Machine tool innovation potential vs. shift to services

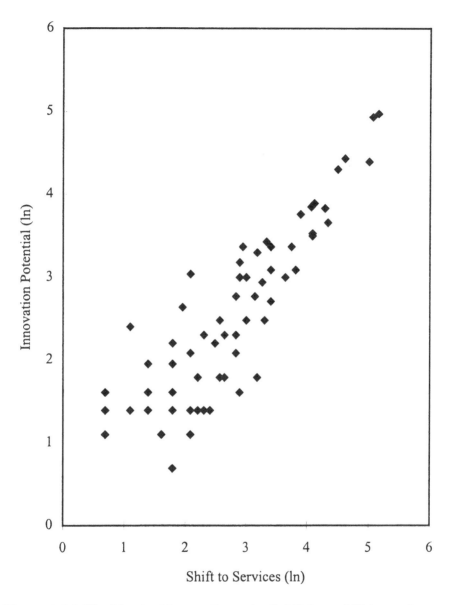

Figure A.14 Machine tool innovation potential (ln) vs. shift to services (ln)

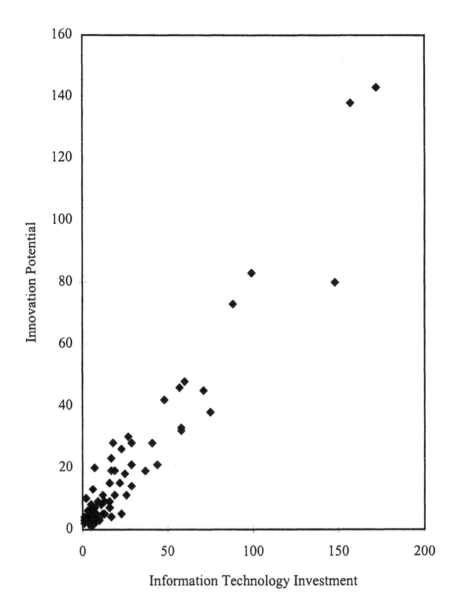

Information Technology Investment

Figure A.15 Machine tool innovation potential vs. information technology investment

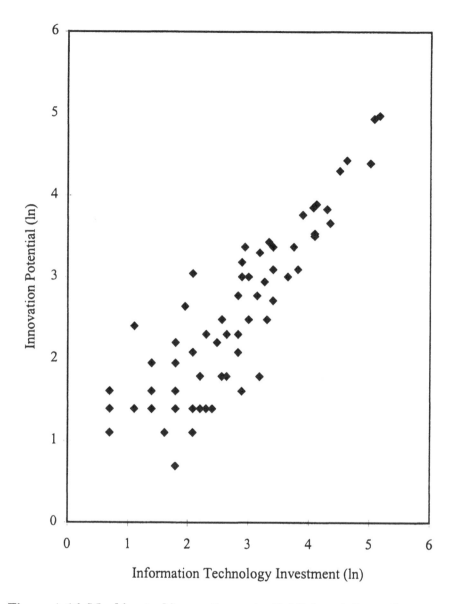

Figure A.16 Machine tool innovation potential (ln) vs. information technology investment (ln)

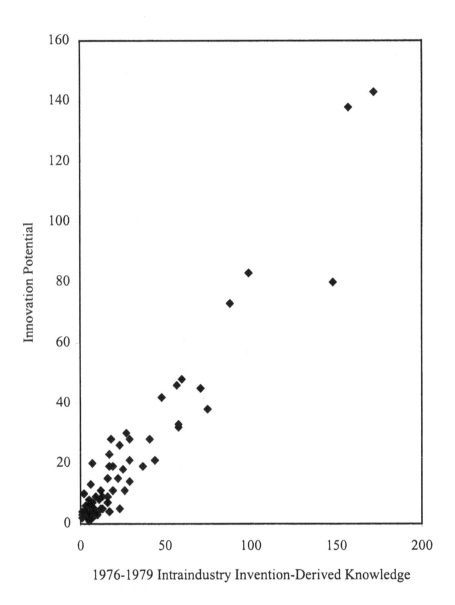

**Figure A.17 Machine tool innovation potential vs. 1976-1979
intraindustry invention-derived knowledge**

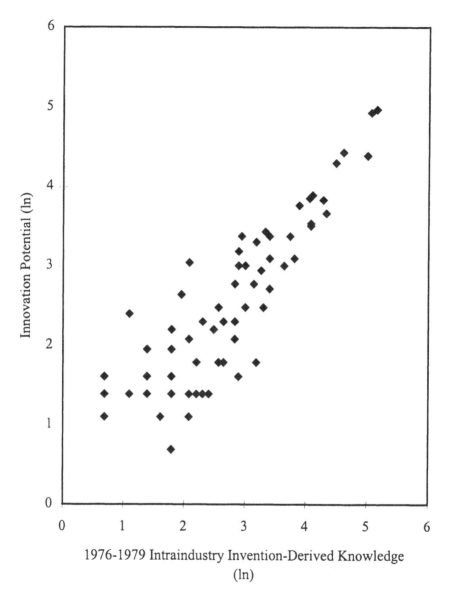

Figure A.18 Machine tool innovation potential (ln) vs. 1976-1979 intraindustry invention-derived knowledge (ln)

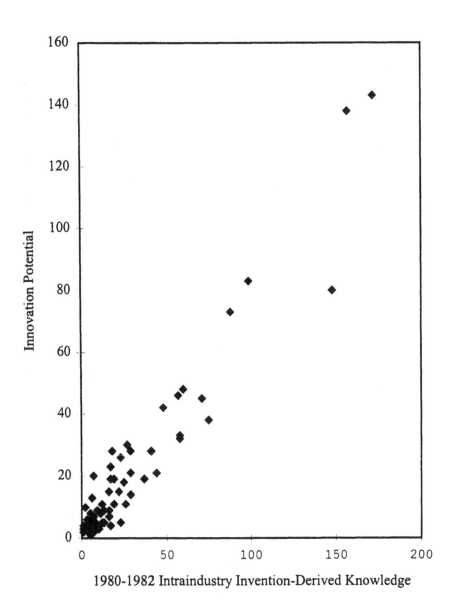

Figure A.19 Machine tool innovation potential vs. 1980-1982 intraindustry invention-derived knowledge

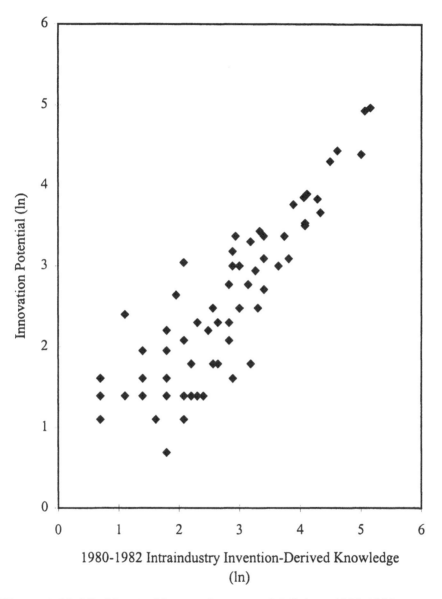

Figure A.20 Machine tool innovation potential (ln) vs. 1980-1982 intraindustry invention-derived knowledge (ln)

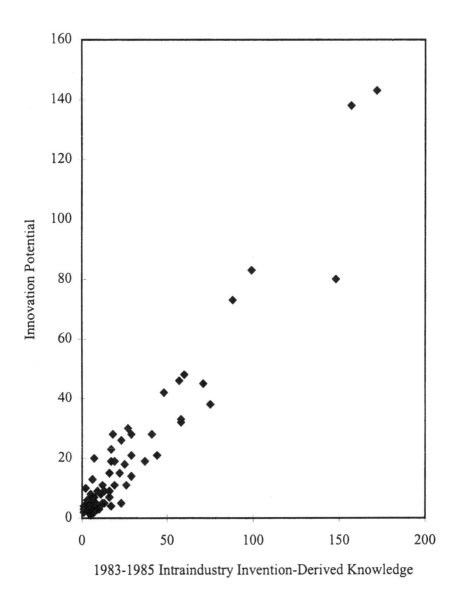

**Figure A.21 Machine tool innovation potential vs. 1983-1985
intraindustry invention-derived knowledge**

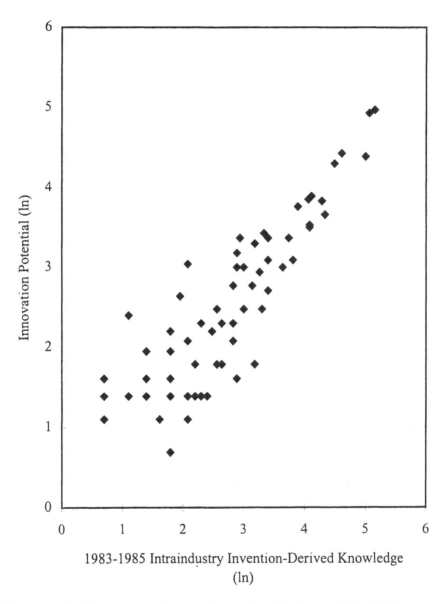

Figure A.22 Machine tool innovation potential (ln) vs. 1983-1985 intraindustry invention-derived knowledge (ln)

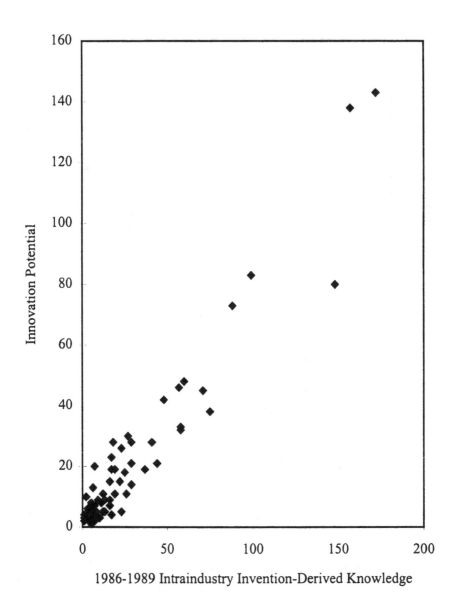

**Figure A.23 Machine tool innovation potential vs. 1986-1989
intraindustry invention-derived knowledge**

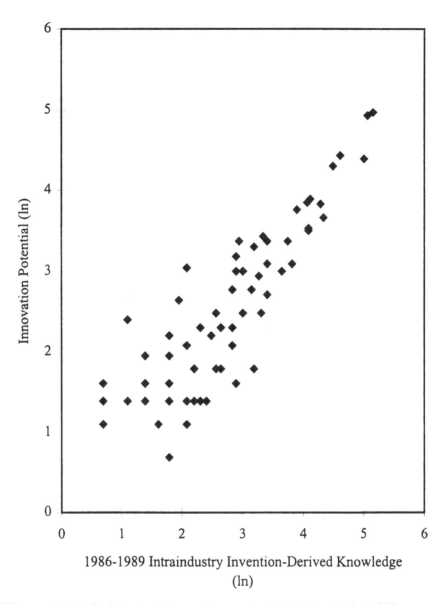

**Figure A.24 Machine tool innovation potential (ln) vs. 1986-1989
intraindustry invention-derived knowledge (ln)**

APPENDIX B

MACHINE TOOL PATENT ACTIVITY OF THE TOP 25 METROPOLITAN AREAS RANKED BY INNOVATION POTENTIAL

Table B.1-Patent activity of the top 25 regions

Rank	Metropolitan Area	FIPS	1976	1977	1978	1979	1980
1	DETROIT, MI	35	38	46	45	27	36
2	LOS ANGELES, CA	49	56	39	53	29	19
3	NEW YORK, NY-NJ	70	37	32	32	27	25
4	CHICAGO, IL-IN-WI	14	36	40	31	26	40
5	Mpls.-St. Paul, MN-WI	5120	8	12	13	6	14
6	PITTSBURGH, PA	78	19	17	14	10	16
7	HOUSTON, TX	42	6	9	12	6	9
8	SAN FRANCISCO, CA	84	13	13	15	11	13
9	BOSTON, MA-NH	7	13	8	13	13	12
10	CLEVELAND, OH	28	21	25	16	11	20
11	Worcester, MA	9243	11	8	10	7	10
12	PHILADELPHIA, PA-NJ-DE	77	9	15	16	10	12
13	SEATTLE, WA	91	6	6	4	6	9
14	San Diego, CA	7320	6	2	6	3	1
15	Raleigh-Durham, NC	6640	0	2	1	1	2
16	PORTLAND, OR-WA	79	6	9	7	5	5
17	HARTFORD, CT	41	14	8	6	7	5
18	Columbus, OH	1840	6	6	8	3	9
19	Rochester, NY	6840	8	3	5	3	8
20	CINCINNATI, OH-KY-IN	21	7	13	7	7	3
21	MILWAUKEE, WI	63	11	9	10	13	11
22	Salt Lake City, UT	7160	0	0	2	0	0
23	Atlanta, GA	520	1	0	3	1	1
24	St. Louis, MO-IL	7040	3	3	6	2	5
25	DALLAS-FT. WORTH, TX	31	2	12	14	9	5

NOTE: Metropolitan areas in all capital letters are CMSAs.

Table B.1-(Continued)

Rank	Metropolitan Area	FIPS	1981	1982	1983	1984	1985
1	DETROIT, MI	35	47	42	28	45	41
2	LOS ANGELES, CA	49	34	32	14	26	40
3	NEW YORK, NY-NJ	70	27	17	18	22	23
4	CHICAGO, IL-IN-WI	14	34	28	25	22	28
5	Mpls.-St. Paul, MN-WI	5120	18	11	8	13	26
6	PITTSBURGH, PA	78	14	14	7	12	10
7	HOUSTON, TX	42	5	7	13	7	12
8	SAN FRANCISCO, CA	84	20	16	8	12	17
9	BOSTON, MA-NH	7	14	14	18	16	19
10	CLEVELAND, OH	28	17	16	8	14	15
11	Worcester, MA	9243	13	9	4	5	4
12	PHILADELPHIA, PA-NJ-DE	77	9	14	15	9	20
13	SEATTLE, WA	91	10	4	6	9	15
14	San Diego, CA	7320	2	5	1	5	3
15	Raleigh-Durham, NC	6640	2	1	2	1	3
16	PORTLAND, OR-WA	79	3	5	3	6	10
17	HARTFORD, CT	41	5	4	7	9	9
18	Columbus, OH	1840	14	5	5	3	7
19	Rochester, NY	6840	10	4	3	3	4
20	CINCINNATI, OH-KY-IN	21	3	6	5	6	11
21	MILWAUKEE, WI	63	13	5	7	12	10
22	Salt Lake City, UT	7160	1	2	0	0	3
23	Atlanta, GA	520	2	3	7	1	4
24	St. Louis, MO-IL	7040	10	5	6	9	8
25	DALLAS-FT. WORTH, TX	31	11	4	2	4	7

NOTE: Metropolitan areas in all capital letters are CMSAs.

Table B.1-(Continued)

Rank	Metropolitan Area	FIPS	1986	1987	1988	1989	1990
1	DETROIT, MI	35	36	38	44	54	47
2	LOS ANGELES, CA	49	39	49	31	38	40
3	NEW YORK, NY-NJ	70	26	20	29	24	23
4	CHICAGO, IL-IN-WI	14	37	38	33	40	24
5	Mpls.-St. Paul, MN-WI	5120	15	22	24	27	29
6	PITTSBURGH, PA	78	21	16	9	14	14
7	HOUSTON, TX	42	11	15	11	20	10
8	SAN FRANCISCO, CA	84	23	15	16	17	15
9	BOSTON, MA-NH	7	11	12	9	16	11
10	CLEVELAND, OH	28	18	22	18	17	9
11	Worcester, MA	9243	6	4	3	4	6
12	PHILADELPHIA, PA-NJ-DE	77	16	10	18	14	7
13	SEATTLE, WA	91	16	12	16	14	10
14	San Diego, CA	7320	7	4	6	10	13
15	Raleigh-Durham, NC	6640	2	3	5	8	9
16	PORTLAND, OR-WA	79	5	7	5	12	5
17	HARTFORD, CT	41	9	10	13	9	5
18	Columbus, OH	1840	3	4	8	8	7
19	Rochester, NY	6840	8	2	5	2	4
20	CINCINNATI, OH-KY-IN	21	9	6	8	6	4
21	MILWAUKEE, WI	63	14	17	7	6	8
22	Salt Lake City, UT	7160	0	1	1	5	5
23	Atlanta, GA	520	3	7	4	3	8
24	St. Louis, MO-IL	7040	2	8	2	7	5
25	DALLAS-FT. WORTH, TX	31	5	12	7	13	8

NOTE: Metropolitan areas in all capital letters are CMSAs.

Table B.1-(Continued)

Rank	Metropolitan Area	FIPS	1991	1992	1976 -92	Innovation Potential
1	DETROIT, MI	35	45	51	710	143
2	LOS ANGELES, CA	49	55	43	637	138
3	NEW YORK, NY-NJ	70	32	28	442	83
4	CHICAGO, IL-IN-WI	14	22	34	538	80
5	Mpls.-St. Paul, MN-WI	5120	24	20	290	73
6	PITTSBURGH, PA	78	18	16	241	48
7	HOUSTON, TX	42	18	18	189	46
8	SAN FRANCISCO, CA	84	11	19	254	45
9	BOSTON, MA-NH	7	14	17	230	42
10	CLEVELAND, OH	28	9	20	276	38
11	Worcester, MA	9243	11	16	131	33
12	PHILADELPHIA, PA-NJ-DE	77	16	10	220	33
13	SEATTLE, WA	91	13	9	165	32
14	San Diego, CA	7320	11	6	91	30
15	Raleigh-Durham, NC	6640	5	14	61	28
16	PORTLAND, OR-WA	79	8	15	116	28
17	HARTFORD, CT	41	13	10	143	28
18	Columbus, OH	1840	10	9	115	26
19	Rochester, NY	6840	8	11	91	23
20	CINCINNATI, OH-KY-IN	21	8	9	118	21
21	MILWAUKEE, WI	63	5	8	166	21
22	Salt Lake City, UT	7160	10	5	35	20
23	Atlanta, GA	520	7	4	59	19
24	St. Louis, MO-IL	7040	8	6	95	19
25	DALLAS-FT. WORTH, TX	31	6	5	126	19

NOTE: Metropolitan areas in all capital letters are CMSAs.

APPENDIX C

BREAKING THE CORRELATION AMONG THE IDK VARIABLES: RESULTS OF INCLUDING ONLY ONE IDK VARIABLE

Table C.1-Breaking the intraindustry IDK correlations

Dependent Variable: Machine Tool Innovation Potential

Variable	Model 1	Model 2
Intercept	-4.110	-3.019
	(-1.251)	(-0.862)
Agglomeration Economies		
Urbanization Economies (ln)	0.008	-0.112
	(0.021)	(-0.297)
Localization Economies (ln)	0.043	0.012
	(0.369)	(0.098)
Federal Government Demand-Pull (ln)	0.016	0.026
	(0.169)	(0.265)
Human Capital		
College Educated (ln)	1.555	0.857
	(1.269)	(0.751)
Graduate Degree (ln)	-1.030	-0.580
	(-1.284)	(-0.780)
Ph.D. Grads. in Mechanical Eng. Produced Locally (ln)	0.252	0.142
	(1.672)	(0.887)
Industrial Restructuring		
Shift to Services (ln)	-0.062	-0.028
	(-0.350)	(-0.159)
Information Technology Investment (ln)	0.282	0.384
	(0.716)	(1.017)
Invention-Derived Knowledge		
Intraindustry		
1976-1979	0.476	-
	(2.138*)	
1980-1982	-	0.532
		(2.092*)
Adjusted R^2	0.613	0.610
df	31	31

*=significance at the 5% level
**=significance at the 1% level
Numbers in parentheses are t-scores

144

Table C.1-(Continued)

Dependent Variable: Machine Tool Innovation Potential

Variable	Model 3	Model 4
Intercept	-4.036	-2.106
	(-1.413)	(-0.824)
Agglomeration Economies		
Urbanization Economies (ln)	0.017	-0.099
	(0.052)	(-0.343)
Localization Economies (ln)	0.060	0.028
	(0.641)	(0.343)
Federal Government Demand-Pull (ln)	-0.020	0.055
	(-0.230)	(0.724)
Human Capital		
College Educated (ln)	1.424	1.551
	(1.375)	(1.740)
Graduate Degree (ln)	-0.164	-0.788
	(-0.251)	(-1.381)
Ph.D. Grads. in Mechanical Eng. Produced Locally (ln)	0.027	0.078
	(0.179)	(0.644)
Industrial Restructuring		
Shift to Services (ln)	-0.034	-0.057
	(-0.222)	(-0.428)
Information Technology Investment (ln)	0.028	0.008
	(0.077)	(0.028)
Invention-Derived Knowledge		
Intraindustry		
1983-1985	0.737	-
	(3.397**)	
1986-1989	-	0.953
		(4.788**)
Adjusted R^2	0.634	0.771
df	31	31

*=significance at the 5% level
**=significance at the 1% level
Numbers in parentheses are t-scores

Table C.2-Breaking the interindustry IDK correlations

Dependent Variable: Machine Tool Innovation Potential

Variable	Model 1	Model 2
Intercept	-4.841	-1.674
	(-1.200)	(-0.385)
Agglomeration Economies		
Urbanization Economies (ln)	-0.145	-0.343
	(-0.346)	(-0.811)
Localization Economies (ln)	0.133	0.092
	(1.070)	(0.805)
Federal Government Demand-Pull (ln)	0.043	0.083
	(0.323)	(0.713)
Human Capital		
College Educated (ln)	0.646	0.393
	(0.521)	(0.336)
Graduate Degree (ln)	-0.654	-0.779
	(-0.699)	(-0.959)
Ph.D. Grads. in Mechanical Eng. Produced Locally (ln)	0.264	0.194
	(1.595)	(1.208)
Industrial Restructuring		
Shift to Services (ln)	0.016	0.003
	(0.084)	(0.015)
Information Technology Investment (ln)	0.628	0.649
	(1.622)	(1.758)
Invention-Derived Knowledge		
Interindustry		
1976-1979	0.095	-
	(0.671)	
1980-1982	-	0.224
		(1.600)
Adjusted R^2	0.542	0.581
df	31	31

*=significance at the 5% level

**=significance at the 1% level

Numbers in parentheses are t-scores

Table C.2-(Continued)

Dependent Variable: Machine Tool Innovation Potential

Variable	Model 3	Model 4
Intercept	-2.443	-2.985
	(-0.594)	(-0.674)
Agglomeration Economies		
Urbanization Economies (ln)	-0.266	-0.273
	(-0.650)	(-0.628)
Localization Economies (ln)	0.054	0.092
	(0.418)	(0.711)
Federal Government Demand-Pull (ln)	0.103	0.067
	(0.821)	(0.539)
Human Capital		
College Educated (ln)	0.665	0.308
	(0.565)	(0.254)
Graduate Degree (ln)	-0.976	-0.608
	(-1.117)	(-0.741)
Ph.D. Grads. in Mechanical Eng. Produced Locally (ln)	0.233	0.220
	(1.474)	(1.348)
Industrial Restructuring		
Shift to Services (ln)	0.040	0.060
	(0.224)	(0.329)
Information Technology Investment (ln)	0.619	0.678
	(1.669)	(1.786)
Invention-Derived Knowledge		
Interindustry		
1983-1985	0.222	-
	(1.537)	
1986-1989	-	0.157
		(1.138)
Adjusted R^2	0.578	0.559
df	31	31

*=significance at the 5% level
**=significance at the 1% level
Numbers in parentheses are t-scores

APPENDIX D

REGIONS INCLUDED IN THE OLS MODELS OF TABLE 5.12

Table D.1-Regions included in models 1-3 of Table 5.12

Metropolitan Area (X indicates region included)	FIPS	Model 1	Model 2	Model 3
BOSTON, MA-NH	7	X	X	X
BUFFALO-NIAGARA FALLS, NY	10	X	X	X
CHICAGO, IL-IN-WI	14	X	X	X
CINCINNATI, OH-KY-IN	21	X	X	X
CLEVELAND, OH	28	X	X	X
DALLAS-FT. WORTH, TX	31	X	X	X
DENVER-BOULDER, CO	34	X	X	X
DETROIT, MI	35	X	X	X
HARTFORD, CT	41	X	X	X
HOUSTON, TX	42	X	X	X
LOS ANGELES, CA	49	X	X	X
MIAMI-FT. LAUDERDALE, FL	56	X	X	X
MILWAUKEE, WI	63	X	X	-
NEW YORK, NY-NJ	70	X	X	X
PHILADELPHIA, PA-NJ-DE	77	X	X	X
PITTSBURGH, PA	78	X	X	X
PORTLAND, OR-WA	79	X	X	-
PROVIDENCE-PAWTUCKET, RI	80	X	-	X
SAN FRANCISCO, CA	84	X	X	X
SEATTLE, WA	91	X	X	X
Albany, NY	160	X	X	X
Albuquerque, NM	200	X	-	-
Atlanta, GA	520	X	X	X
Baltimore, MD	720	X	X	X
Charlotte, NC	1520	X	X	-
Columbia, SC	1760	X	-	X

NOTE: Metropolitan areas in all capital letters are CMSAs.

149

Table D.1-(Continued)

Metropolitan Area (X indicates region included)	FIPS	Model 1	Model 2	Model 3
Columbus, OH	1840	X	X	X
Dayton, OH	2000	X	X	-
Flint, MI	2640	X	-	-
Grand Rapids, MI	3000	X	X	-
Greensboro, NC	3120	X	X	-
Indianapolis, IN	3480	X	X	-
Kansas City, MO	3760	X	X	-
Knoxville, TN	3840	X	-	X
Louisville, KY	4520	X	X	-
Minneapolis-St. Paul, MN	5120	X	X	X
New Orleans, LA	5560	X	X	X
Norfolk, VA	5720	X	X	X
Omaha, NE	5920	X	-	-
Orlando, FL	5960	X	X	-
Phoenix, AZ	6200	X	X	X
Raleigh-Durham, NC	6640	X	X	X
Richmond, VA	6760	X	X	-
Rochester, NY	6840	X	X	X
Sacramento, CA	6920	X	X	X
St. Louis, MO	7040	X	X	X
Salt Lake City, UT	7160	X	X	X
San Diego, CA	7320	X	X	X
Springfield, MA	8003	X	-	X
Syracuse, NY	8160	X	-	X
Tampa, FL	8280	X	X	-
Toledo, OH	8400	X	-	X
Tucson, AZ	8520	X	-	X
Washington, DC	8840	X	X	X
West Palm Beach, FL	8960	X	X	-

NOTE: Metropolitan areas in all capital letters are CMSAs.

Table D.2-Regions included in models 4-6 of Table 5.12

Metropolitan Area (X indicates region included)	FIPS	Model 1	Model 2	Model 3
BOSTON, MA-NH	7	X	X	X
CHICAGO, IL-IN-WI	14	X	X	X
CLEVELAND, OH	28	X	X	X
DALLAS-FT. WORTH, TX	31	X	X	X
DENVER-BOULDER, CO	34	X	X	X
DETROIT, MI	35	X	X	X
HARTFORD, CT	41	X	X	X
HOUSTON, TX	42	X	X	X
LOS ANGELES, CA	49	X	X	X
NEW YORK, NY-NJ	70	X	X	X
PHILADELPHIA, PA-NJ-DE	77	X	X	X
PITTSBURGH, PA	78	X	X	X
SAN FRANCISCO, CA	84	X	X	X
SEATTLE, WA	91	X	X	X
Albany, NY	160	X	X	X
Albuquerque, NM	200	X	-	-
Atlanta, GA	520	X	X	X
Austin, TX	640	X	X	X
Baltimore, MD	720	X	X	X
Dayton, OH	2000	X	X	X
Greensboro, NC	3120	X	X	-
Indianapolis, IN	3480	X	X	-
Kansas City, MO	3760	X	X	-
Knoxville, TN	3840	X	-	X
Minneapolis-St. Paul, MN	5120	X	X	X
Orlando, FL	5960	X	X	X
Phoenix, AZ	6200	X	X	X
Raleigh-Durham, NC	6640	X	X	X
Rochester, NY	6840	X	X	X
Sacramento, CA	6920	X	X	X
St. Louis, MO	7040	X	X	X
Salt Lake City, UT	7160	X	X	X
San Antonio, TX	7240	X	X	-
San Diego, CA	7320	X	X	X
Syracuse, NY	8160	X	-	X
Tucson, AZ	8520	X	-	X
Tulsa, OK	8560	X	X	-
Washington, DC	8840	X	X	X
West Palm Beach, FL	8960	X	X	X

NOTE: Metropolitan areas in all capital letters are CMSAs.

151

Bibliography

Abernathy, W.J. and B.S. Chakravarthy. 1979. Government innovation and innovation in industry: A policy framework. *Sloan Management Review* 20: 3-18.

Abernathy, William J. and James M. Utterback. 1978. Patterns of industrial innovation. *Technology Review* 80 (June\July): 40-47.

Acs, Zoltan J. and David B. Audretsch. 1987. Innovation, market structure, and firm size. *The Review of Economics and Statistics* 69 (November): 567-574.

_____. 1988. Innovation in large and small firms: An empirical analysis. *American Economic Review* 78 (September): 678-690.

_____. 1989. Patents as a measure of innovative activity. *Kyklos* 42: 171-180.

Allen, T.J., J.M. Utterback, M.A. Sirbu, N.A. Ashford and J.H. Holloman. 1978. Government influence on the innovation process. *Research Policy* 7: 124-149.

Allison, Paul D., J. Scott Long and Tad K. Krauze. 1982. Cumulative advantage and inequality in science. *American Sociological Review* 47 (October): 615-625.

Arthur, W. Brian. 1990. Positive feedbacks in the economy. *Scientific American* 262 (February): 92-99.

Ashburn, Anderson. 1988. The machine tool industry: The crumbling foundation. In, *Is New Technology Enough? Making and Remaking U.S. Basic Industries*, (ed.) Donald A. Hicks, 19-85. Washington, D.C. American Enterprise Institute for Public Policy Research.

Bartel, Ann P. and Frank R. Lichtenberg. 1987. The comparative advantage of educated workers in implementing new technology. *Review of Economics and Statistics* 69 (February): 1-11.

Basberg, B.L. 1987. Patents and the measurement of technological change: A survey of the literature. *Research Policy* 16: 131-141.

Bean, A.S. and N.R. Baker. 1988. Implementing national innovation policies through private decisionmaking. In, *Government Innovation Policy: Design, Implementation, Evaluation*, (ed.) J.D. Roessner, 75-89. New York: St. Martin's Press.

Beeson, Patricia. 1987. Total factor productivity growth and agglomeration economies in manufacturing, 1959-73. *Journal of Regional Science 27*: 183-199.

Beggs, John J. 1984. Long-run trends in patenting. In, *R&D, Patents, and Productivity*, (ed.) Zvi Griliches, 155-173. Chicago: University of Chicago Press.

Berry, Brian J.L. 1972. Hierarchical diffusion: The basis of developmental filtering and spread in a system of growth centres. In, *Growth Centres in Regional Economic Development*, (ed.) Niles M. Hansen, 108-138. New York: Free Press.

_____. 1973. *Growth Centers in the American Urban System*. Cambridge, MA: Ballinger Publishing Company.

_____, Edgar C. Conkling and D. Michael Ray. 1987. *Economic Geography*. Englewood Cliffs, N.J.: Prentice-Hall.

_____. 1991. *Long-Wave Rhythms in Economic Development and Political Behavior*. Baltimore: The Johns Hopkins University Press.

Boitani, A. and E. Ciciotti. 1990. Patents as indicators of innovative performance at the regional level. In, *The Spatial Context of Technological Development*, (eds.) R. Cappelin and P. Nijkamp, 139-163. Aldershot: Gower.

Borrus, M.G. 1988. *Competing for Control: America's Stake in Microelectronics*. Cambridge, MA: Ballinger Publishing Company.

Brugger, E.A. and B. Stuckey. 1987. Regional economic structure and innovative behavior in Switzerland. *Regional Studies* 21: 241-251.

Burgan, John U. 1985. Cyclical behavior of high tech industries. *Monthly Labor Review* 108 (May): 9-15.

Carlino, Gerald A. 1979. Increasing returns to scale in metropolitan manufacturing. *Journal of Regional Science* 19: 363-373.

_____. 1987. Productivity in cities: Does city size matter? *Business Review, Federal Reserve Bank of Philadelphia* (November/December): 3-12.

_____. 1993. Highways and education: The road to productivity? *Business Review, Federal Reserve Bank of Philadelphia* (September/October): 21-31.

_____ and Richard Voith. 1992. Accounting for differences in aggregate state productivity. *Regional Science and Urban Economics* 2 (December): 597-617.

The Chicago shows. *American Machinist*, 19 October 1970: 105-124.

Coffey, W.J. and M. Polese. 1987. Trade and location of producer services: A Canadian perspective. *Environment and Planning A* 19 (May): 597-611.

Comanor, W. and F.M. Scherer. 1969. Patent statistics as a measure of technical change. *Journal of Political Economy* 77: 329-398.

Czmanzki, Stanley and L.A. de Q. Ablas. 1979. Identification of industrial clusters and complexes. *Urban Studies* 16: 61-80.

Davelaar, Evert and Peter Nijkamp. 1989. The role of metropolitan milieu as an incubator center for technological innovations: A Dutch case study. *Urban Studies* 26: 516-529.

Dertouzos, Michael L., Richard K. Lester, Robert M. Solow and The MIT Commission on Industrial Productivity. 1989. *Made in America: Regaining the Productive Edge*. Cambridge, Massachusetts: The MIT Press.

DiFilippo, Anthony. 1986. *Military Spending and Industrial Decline: A Study of the American Machine Tool Industry*. New York: Greenwood Press.

Dorfman, Nancy S. 1983. Route 128: The development of a regional high technology economy. *Research Policy* 12: 299-316.

Dosi, Giovanni. 1988. The nature of the innovative process. In, *Technical Change and Economic Theory*, (eds.) Giovanni Dosi, Christopher Freeman, Richard Nelson, Gerald Silverberg and Luc Soete, 221-238. London: Pinter Publishers.

Fagerberg, Jan. 1994. Technology and International Differences in Growth Rates. *Journal of Economic Literature* 32 (September): 1147-1175.

Feldman, Maryann P. 1992. The geography of innovation: A cross sectional analysis of state level data. Ph.D. diss., Carnegie-Mellon University.

Finegold, David, Keith W. Brendley, Robert Lempert, Donald Henry, Peter Cannon, Brent Boultinghouse and Max Nelson. 1994. *The Decline of the U.S. Machine Tool Industry and Prospects for Its Sustainable Recovery*. Santa Monica: RAND.

Flamm, K. 1987. *Targeting the Computer: Government Support and International Competition*. Washington, D.C.: Brookings Institution.

Florida, Richard, and Martin Kenney. 1990. *The Breakthrough Illusion: Corporate America's Failure to Move from Innovation to Mass Production*. New York: Basic Books.

Foray, D., M. Gibbons and G. Ferne. 1989. *Major R&D Programmes for Information Technology*. Paris: OECD.

Future perfect? A survey of Silicon Valley. *The Economist*, 29 March 1997, 1-20.

Gilbert, Anne. 1988. The new regional geography in English and French-speaking countries. *Progress in Human Geography* 12: 208-228.

Goldberger, Marvin L., Brendan A. Maher and Pamela Ebert Flattau, (eds.) 1995. *Research-Doctorate Programs in the United States: Continuity and Change*. Washington, D.C.: National Academy Press.

Goodall, Brian. 1972. *The Economics of Urban Areas*. Oxford: Pergamon Press.

Greene, William H. 1993. *Econometric Analysis*. 2nd ed. Englewood Cliffs, N.J.: Prentice-Hall.

Grefsheim, Suzanne, Jon Franklin and Diana Cunningham. 1991. Biotechnology awareness study, part 1: Where scientists get their information. *Bulletin of the Medical Library Association* 79 (January): 36-44.

Griffin, K. 1978. *International Inequality and National Poverty*. London: Macmillan.

Griliches, Zvi. 1957. Hybrid corn: An exploration in the economics of technological change. *Econometrica* 25: 501-522.

_____. 1979. Issues in assessing the contribution of R&D to productivity growth. *Bell Journal of Economics* 10 (Spring): 92-116.

_____. 1990. Patent statistics as economic indicators: A survey. *The Journal of Economic Literature* 28 (December): 1661-1707.

155

_____, Ariel Pakes and B.H. Hall. 1987. The value of patents as indicators of inventive activity. In, *Economic Policy and Technological Performance*, (eds.) P. Dasgupta and P. Stoneman, 97-124. Cambridge: Cambridge University Press.

Grossman, Gene M. and Elhanan Helpman. 1994. Endogenous innovation in the theory of growth. *Journal of Economic Perspectives*. 8 (Winter): 23-44.

Gujarati, Damodar N. 1988. *Basic Econometrics*. 2nd ed. New York: McGraw-Hill Book Company.

Hagerstrand, Torsten. 1967. *Innovation Diffusion as a Spatial Process*. Translated by Allan Pred. Chicago: University of Chicago Press.

Hall, George E. and Courtenay M. Slater, (eds.) 1996. *1996 County and City Extra: Annual Metro, City and County Data Book*. Lanham, Maryland: Bernan Press.

Hicks, Donald A. and Si-Gyoung Lee. 1994. Regional economic impacts of federal R&D by funding source and performer type. *Regional Studies* 28: 619-632.

Hicks, Donald A. and Steven R. Nivin. 1993. Industrial and demographic restructuring and economic performance: The tertiary crisis revisited. Paper presented at the Annual Meeting of the Western Regional Science Association, Houston, Tx., 12-14 November.

_____. 1994. Regional returns to capital diversity: Decoupling and Appropriation. Paper presented at the Annual Meeting of the Western Regional Science Association, Tucson, Az., 23-27 February.

_____. 1995. Spillover and appropriation: Economic returns to regional investments and endowments. U.T.D. Political Economy Working Paper 95-23 (July): 1-25.

_____. 1996. Global credentials, immigration, and metro-regional economic performance. *Urban Geography* 17 (January 1-February 14): 23-43.

Hicks, Donald A. and John Rees. 1993. Cities and beyond: A new look at the nation's urban economy. In, *Rediscovering Urban America: Perspectives on the 1980s*, (eds.) Jack Sommer and Donald A. Hicks, 2.1-2.125. Washington, D.C.: U.S. Department of Housing and Urban Development Office of Policy Development and Research.

Jacobs, Jane. 1969. *The Economy of Cities*. New York: Random House.

Jaffe, Adam B. 1986. Technological opportunity and spillovers of R&D: Evidence from firms' patents, profits, and market value. *American Economic Review* 76 (December): 984-1001.

_____. 1989. Real effects of academic research. *American Economic Review* 79 (December): 957-970.

Judge, George G., W.E. Griffiths, R. Carter Hill, Helmut Lutkepohl, Tsoung-Chao Lee. 1985. *The Theory and Practice of Econometrics*. 2nd ed. New York: John Wiley and Sons.

Kaldor, Nicholas. 1970. The case for regional policies. *Scottish Journal of Political Economy* 17 (November): 337-347.

Kash, D.E. 1989. *Perpetual Innovation: The New World of Competition*. New York: Basic Books.

Kawashima, Tatsuhiko. 1975. Urban agglomeration economies in manufacturing industries. *Papers of the Regional Science Association* 34: 157-175.

Kline, Stephen J. and Nathan Rosenberg. 1986. An overview of innovation. In, *The Positive-Sum Strategy: Harnessing Technology for Economic Growth*, (eds.) Ralph Landau and Nathan Rosenberg, 275-305. Washington, D.C.: National Academy of Sciences.

Kmenta, Jan. 1986. *Elements of Econometrics*. 2nd ed. New York: Macmillan Publishing Company.

Krugman, Paul. 1991. *Geography and Trade*. Cambridge, MA: The MIT Press.

Labich, Kenneth. 1993. The best cities for knowledge workers. *Fortune*, 15 November, 50-78.

Landau, Ralph. 1988. U.S. economic growth. *Scientific American* 258 (June): 44-52.

Levin, Richard C. 1982. The semiconductor industry. In, *Government and Technical Progress: A Cross-Industry Analysis*, (ed.) Richard R. Nelson, 9-100. New York: Pergamon Press.

Levin, Richard C., Wesley M. Cohen and David C. Mowery. 1985. R&D appropriability, opportunity, and market structure: New evidence on some Schumpeterian hypotheses. *American Economic Review* 75 (May): 20-24.

MacPherson, A. 1991. Interfirm information linkages in an economically disadvantaged region: An empirical perspective from metropolitan Buffalo. *Environment and Planning A* 23 (April): 591-606.

Maidique M.A. and R.H. Hayes. 1984. The art of high-technology management. *Sloan Management Review* 25: 17-31.

Malecki, Edward J. 1984. Military spending and the US defense industry: Regional patterns of military contracts and subcontracts. *Environment and Planning C: Government and Policy* 2: 31-44.

_____. 1991. *Technology and Economic Development.* New York: John Wiley and Sons, Inc.

Mansfield, Edwin. 1968. *The Economics of Technological Change.* New York: W.W. Norton.

_____. 1981. Composition of R and D Expenditures: Relationship to size of firm, concentration, and innovative output. *Review of Economics and Statistics* 63 (November): 610-615.

_____. 1991. Academic research and industrial innovation. *Research Policy* 20 (February): 1-12.

The manufacturing myth. *The Economist*, 19 March 1994, 91-92.

Markusen, Ann. 1987. *Regions: The Economics and Politics of Territory.* Totowa, New Jersey: Rowman and Allanheld.

Markusen, Ann, Peter Hall and Amy Glasmeier. 1986. *High Tech America.* Boston: Allen and Unwin.

McArthur, R. 1990. Replacing the concept of high technology: Towards a diffusion-based approach. *Environment and Planning A* 22 (June): 811-828.

Mehay, Stephen L. and Loren M. Solnick. 1990. Defense spending and state economic growth. *Journal of Regional Science* 30 (Novemebr): 477-487.

Metalworking: Yesterday and tomorrow. *American Machinist,* November 1977, B1-C17.

Meyer, John. 1963. Regional economics: A survey. *American Economic Review* 53: 19-54.

Mills, Edwin S. and Bruce W. Hamilton. 1989. *Urban Economics.* 4th ed. Glenview, IL: Scott, Foresman and Company.

Molina, A.H. 1989. *The Social Basis of the Microelectronics Revolution.* Edinburgh: Edinburgh University Press.

Morrill, Richard L. 1968. Waves of spatial diffusion. *Journal of Regional Science* 8 (Summer): 1-18.

158

Myers, S. and D.G. Marquis. 1969. *Successful Industrial Innovation.* Washington, D.C.: National Science Foundation.

Narin F., E. Noma and R. Perry. 1987. Patents as indicators of corporate technological strength. *Research Policy* 16: 143-155.

Neff R., P. Magnusson and W.J. Holstein. 1989. Rethinking Japan. *Business Week*, 7 August, 15-22.

Nelson, Richard R. 1982. Government stimulus of technological progress: Lessons from American history. In, *Government and Technical Progress: A Cross-Industry Study*, (ed.) Richard R. Nelson, 451-482. New York: Pergamon Press.

_____. 1984. *High-technology Policies: A Five-Nation Comparison.* Washington: American Enterprise Institute.

_____. 1986. Institutions supporting technical advance in industry. *American Economic Review* 76 (May): 186-189.

_____. 1996. *The Sources of Economic Growth.* Cambridge, MA: Harvard University Press.

1972 international machine tool show report. *American Machinist*, 18 September 1972: 69-80.

Noyelle, Thierry J. and Thomas M. Stanback, Jr. 1984. *The Economic Transformation of American Cities.* Totowa, N.J.: Rowman and Allanheld.

OECD. 1986. *OECD Science and Technology Indicators, No. 2: R&D, Invention and Competitiveness.* Paris: Organisation for Economic Co-operation and Development.

Ogburn, William F. 1933. The influence of invention and discovery. In, *Recent Social Trends in the United States: Report of the President's Research Committee on Social Trends*, 122-166. New York: McGraw-Hill.

Pakes, Ariel and Zvi Griliches. 1984. Patents and R&D at the firm's level: A first look. In, *R&D, Patents, and Productivity*, (ed.) Zvi Griliches, 55-72. Chicago: University of Chicago Press.

Pedersen, Paul Ove. 1970. Innovation diffusion within and between national urban systems. *Geographical Analysis* 2 (July): 203-254.

Porter, Michael E. 1990. *The Competitive Advantage of Nations.* New York: The Free Press.

Pred, Allen R. 1966. *The Spatial Dynamics of U.S. Urban-Industrial Growth, 1800-1914.* Cambridge, MA: The MIT Press.

Quinn, James Brian. 1986. The impacts of technology in the services sector. In, *Technology and Global Industry: Companies and Nations in the World Economy*, (eds.) Bruce R. Guile and Harvey Brooks, 119-159. Washington, D.C.: National Academy of Engineering.

Rees, J. 1987. What happened to macroeconomics? *Environment and Planning A* 19: 139-141.

Rendeiro, Joao O. 1985. How the Japanese came to dominate the machine tool industry. *Long Range Planning* 18: 62-67.

Richardson, Harry W. 1973. *Regional Growth Theory*. New York: John Wiley and Sons.

_____. 1978. *Urban Economics*. Hinsdale, IL: The Dryden Press.

Riche, Richard W., Daniel E. Hecker and John U. Burgan. 1983. High technology today and tomorrow: A small slice of the employment pie. *Monthly Labor Review* 106 (November): 50-58.

Robinson, Edward A. 1996. American toolmakers regain their cutting edge. *Fortune*, 10 June, 72[C]-72[N].

Roessner, J.D. 1987. Technology policy in the United States: Structures and limitations. *Technovation* 5: 229-245.

Romer, Paul M. 1986. Increasing returns and long-run growth. *Journal of Political Economy* 94: 1002-1037.

_____. 1994. The origins of endogenous growth. *Journal of Economic Perspectives* 8 (Winter): 3-22.

Rosenberg, Nathan. 1963. Technological change in the machine tool industry, 1840-1910. *The Journal of Economic History* 23 (December): 414-446.

_____. 1974. Science, invention, and economic growth. *The Economic Journal* 84 (March): 90-108.

_____. 1982. *Inside the Black Box: Technology and Economics*. New York: Cambridge University Press.

_____. 1986. The impact of technological innovation: A historical view. In, *The Positive Sum Strategy: Harnessing Technology for Economic Growth*, (eds.) Ralph Landau and Nathan Rosenberg, 17-32. Washington, D.C.: National Academy Press.

_____. 1994. *Exploring the Black Box*. Cambridge, Great Britain: Cambridge University Press.

Rosenberg, Nathan and Richard R. Nelson. 1994. American universities and technical advance in industry. *Research Policy* 23: 323-348.

Rothwell, R. 1980. The impact of regulation on innovation: Some U.S. data. *Technological Forecasting and Social Change* 17: 7-34.

Scherer, F.M. 1982. Inter-industry technology flows and productivity growth. *Review of Economics and Statistics* 64 (December): 627-634.

_____. 1983. The propensity to patent. *International Journal of Industrial Organization* 1: 107-128.

Schmookler, Jacob. 1966. *Invention and Economic Growth*. Cambridge, MA: Harvard University Press.

Schumpeter, Joseph A. 1950. *Capitalism, Socialism and Democracy*. New York: Harper & Row, Publishers.

Shefer, Daniel. 1973. Localization economies in SMSAs: A production function analysis. *Journal of Regional Science* 13 (April): 55-64.

Segal, David. 1976. Are there returns to scale in city size? *Review of Economics and Statistics* 58: 339-350.

Solow, Robert M. 1957. Technical change and the aggregate production function. *Review of Economics and Statistics* 39: 312-320.

Stewart, F. 1978. *Technology and Underdevelopment*. 2nd ed. London: Macmillan.

Suarez-Villa, Luis. 1993. The dynamics of regional invention and innovation: Innovative capacity and regional change in the twentieth century. *Geographical Analysis* 25 (April): 147-164.

_____ and Syed A. Hasnath. 1993. The effect of infrastructure on invention: Innovative capacity and the dynamics of public construction investment. *Technological Forecasting and Social Change* 44 (December): 333-358.

Survey: Manufacturing technology. *The Economist*, 5 March 1994, 1-18.

Sveikauskas, Leo. 1975. The productivity of cities. *Quarterly Journal of Economics* 89: 393-413.

Thompson, Chris. 1988. Some problems with R&D/SE&T-based definitions of high technology industry. *Area* 20: 265-277.

U.S. Patent and Trademark Office. 1992. *Technology Profile Report: Semiconductor Devices and Manufacture, 1/1963-12/1991*. Washington, D.C.: U.S. Patent and Trademark Office.

_____. 1993. *Technology Profile Report: Machine Tools - Metal Working, 1/1963-12/1992.* Washington, D.C.: U.S. Patent and Trademark Office.

von Boventer, Edwin. 1970. Optimal spatial structure and regional development. *Kyklos* 23: 903-926.

Wagoner, Harless D. 1968. *The U.S. Machine Tool Industry from 1900 to 1950.* Cambridge, MA: MIT Press.

Westphal, Larry E. 1987. Industrial development in East Asia's "gang of four." *Issues in Science and Technology* 3 (Spring): 78-88.

What computers are for. *The Economist,* 22 January 1994, 74.

Where are the jobs?. *The Economist,* 22 May 1993, 327.

Winter, Sidney G. 1984. Schumpeterian competition in alternative technological regimes. *Journal of Economic Behavior and Organization* 5 (September-December): 287-320.

Workers of the world unite. *The Economist,* 23 October 1993, 88.

Wozniak, Gregory D. 1987. Human capital, information, and early adoption of new technology. *Journal of Human Resources* 22 (Winter): 101-112.